PURSUIT

PURSUIT

LIVING FULLY IN SEARCH OF GOD'S PRESENCE

SCOTT CHROSTEK

The House Studio

PO Box 419527

Kansas City, MO 64141

Copyright 2012 by Scott Chrostek

ISBN 978-0-8341-2832-3

Printed in the United States of America

Cover Design: Brandon Hill

Interior Design: Sharon Page

www.thehousestudio.com

10 9 8 7 6 5 4 3 2 1

CONTENTS

FOREWORD

Missional living starts with a fundamental conviction that each day is a gift from God, that each encounter with another is an opportunity for God to use us, that God speaks if we'll only listen, and that God's mission field is our everyday life. We awaken each day remembering that we are called to be salt and light. We look at each person we meet as a child of God. We step out of our homes saying, "Here I am, Lord; use me!" Worship is not something confined to the four walls of a church building but what happens when we seek to give glory to God each day. Service is not something we sign up to do for an hour a week, but it is our fundamental orientation in life. We don't do mission on a mission trip. We are sent forth on God's mission every day.

Scott Chrostek gets this. He walks out the door of his home each day anticipating God is at work: his task is to make himself available and to pay attention.

I met Scott in the fall of 2006 while at a banquet in Detroit. I was speaking on the importance of new church development. He was attending the banquet, hoping it would end early so he could catch his beloved Detroit Tigers playing the Cards in the World Series. I had no idea he was such a huge Tigers fan, and I asked if he and his wife, Wendy, would want to join me for coffee after the dinner. We sat and talked about their hopes and dreams for starting a new church or redeveloping an old one. Never once did he let on what a huge

Tigers fan he was or how much he wished he could be watching the big game. He wouldn't let on about this because he was paying attention, wondering if God was somehow at work in our meeting.

That night we began a friendship that ultimately resulted in Scott and Wendy joining our staff at the Church of the Resurrection, where Wendy serves on our congregational care team and Scott launched and leads Resurrection Downtown. Kansas City is different because of Scott's work in the heart of the city. Lives have been changed. People have come to faith. God's mission is being accomplished. And this happened because Scott was willing to have a cup of coffee while his favorite sports team was playing in the World Series.

In two years the church—not in a bustling suburb, but in the heart of our city—has grown from a handful of people to over six hundred in weekly attendance. His charisma, strong relationship-building skills, passionate faith, and wisdom that is beyond his years have helped attract a diverse and exciting group of people to the church. Scott is also a gifted preacher who serves as the primary preaching voice when I'm out of the pulpit at the Church of the Resurrection.

Beyond this, what is so compelling about Scott is that he preaches and practices the missional life he writes about in this book. He does so in an utterly contagious way that draws others into a deeper relationship with God. Scott describes the missional life as one in which the person who is living it "sees the world and everything in it as a gift and opportunity to meet and experience God's perfect love" and to share it with everyone you meet, in every situation, in all you do.

Scott's descriptions of the seven dimensions of a missional life are compelling, inviting, and inspiring. I believe all who read this book will find themselves longing to pursue God and his mission for their lives.

—Adam Hamilton
Senior Pastor
The United Methodist Church of the Resurrection

ACKNOWLEDGMENTS

I am deeply grateful to Chris Folmsbee for the invitation to write this book. It has been an honor and privilege. Chris's friendship, encouragement, and guidance throughout this process have been an absolute blessing.

I wish also to thank those who have shared in the formation of this project as it has emerged over the past two years. I am especially thankful for all of those unexpected people who I have met and fell in love with along the way. You are the people and yours are the stories that have offered me glimpses of God in real life. To the congregations I have been privileged to serve and to my friends in North Carolina, Kentucky, Brighton, and Detroit: you have helped me become the person I am today.

This book would not have been possible without the people of the Church of the Resurrection Downtown and their willingness to afford me the space and time to write this book. I am especially thankful for those of you who helped me find the words: David and Kelly Sisney, Shawn Stogsdill, Paul Haddix, and Josh Knight.

Several people kindly read parts or all of the manuscript and have even helped me knock off some of its corners: Laceye Warner, Bishop Robert Schnase, Adam Hamilton, Mike Slaughter, and Lovett Weems. Thank you for your wisdom, generosity, and grace.

I wrote this book shortly after Resurrection Downtown had determined to purchase a permanent space in downtown Kansas City. As a part of our capital campaign, all of the proceeds from this book are being directed toward our new building, a renovated bar/concert venue that sits in the center of the city between a strip club and tattoo parlor. From the time we moved in, our community has experienced rapid growth and amazing transformation. In twenty-four months we have grown from nine to over six hundred in weekly worship. In the first six months at our new space we have participated in over sixty-five baptisms, fifty-two of whom were adults. God has indeed blessed us. God's Spirit is certainly alive. My hope is that this book captures the spirit and energy of what has been happening in downtown Kansas City.

Lastly, I want to express appreciation to my wife, Wendy, for being willing to push me, support me, encourage me, and ground me, all while loving me. I am thankful for the first day she asked me to share a meal with her in North Carolina, and I'm thankful for her now. She has invited and accompanied me into more life-changing experiences than I could have ever imagined. I am blessed to have her at every table as my companion and partner.

INTRODUCTION

Before we begin, here's a little bit about me . . .

I'm thirty-two years old. I've been married for seven of those years to a wonderful woman named Wendy, and together we have a dog named Ellie. While my wife is from southwest Louisiana, I am proudly imported from Detroit. I love the Detroit Tigers and the Detroit Red Wings, and unfortunately, I am reluctantly supportive and hopelessly devoted to the Detroit Lions. I feel similarly about Ford, GM, and Fiat (formerly known as Chrysler).

More than anything, I would consider myself a millennial with a touch of Generation X.

I am a product of the eighties. I grew up watching the likes of Bill Cosby, Kirk Cameron (before he was a Christian), and Michael J. Fox, who I knew as Alex P. Keaton from *Family Ties*. Alex P. Keaton was my role model. I wanted to be just like him. In middle school I wore a sweater vest and tie. In high school I carried around copies of the *Wall Street Journal*, and from the early age of twelve I began dreaming of the day when I would end up on the trading floor of the New York Stock Exchange.

I came pretty close to Wall Street, but at the age of twenty-six, after making my way through degrees at both the University of Michigan (Go Blue!) and Duke University (Go Devils!), a career in investments, and several different states, I became an ordained elder in the Detroit Annual Conference of the United Methodist Church. I am now a pastor.

For the past two years I have been serving as pastor on loan from Detroit, a shrinking city, in order to serve the church in Kansas City, a growing city. I moved to Kansas City to plant a church in the heart of a city, known not for its baseball, hockey, or cars but for its basketball, BBQ, and stockyards. Our church has grown from 9 people to over 650 people in the last two years.

In addition to planting a church in Kansas City, I have also found myself serving in three different annual conferences of the United Methodist Church. That makes me one of the only, if not the only, clergyperson in the United Methodist Church who is working for six bosses (three bishops and three district superintendents). I am a living example of a real-life *Office Space*. If I ever mess up, I will hear about it six times. All of this is to say that being a pastor was never something I imagined doing. I never saw it coming.

The Pursuit of the Missional Life

Most of the people I spend time with these days feel as though they are trapped. They are typically professional men and women, both young and old, who feel limited or shackled by their professions, incomes, and careers. Their dreams of pathways, once unlimited, are now limited to the predictable steps of their corporate ladders. I meet people who are working at jobs that were supposed to provide them with a sense of meaning and identity, but after a few years or maybe several months, they have realized this is not the case. Their Wall Streets have led them to a place where the streets have no name. So they wander. They are longing for something. They are searching for meaning, purpose, and fulfillment. They are searching for what I call the missional life. They want to pursue God but do not know how.

Does this sound familiar?

Is this you?

This was me.

At twenty-four years old I left a successful career leading me toward Wall Street in order to pursue an entirely different kind of life. In the days, months, and years leading up to this decision, I felt empty and alone. I wanted more. I wasn't satisfied with my accomplishments, my income, or my responsibilities. I felt as if I had more to offer the world, but I didn't know how to give or what to do.

Bubbling within me was the fear that I would never be satisfied with my life. I remember thinking that I would never be able to live fully until I fully owned who I was or until I finally claimed the person I believed God had created me to be. What troubled me the most, however, was that I felt God calling me into full-time ministry. Working alongside high net worth individuals, I secretly knew that I wasn't going to be happy until I left everything I was and all that I had in order to live fully as the person I was created to be.

Making that move and changing my course has transformed my life, but what I've learned since then is that not everyone is called to abandon their career or all that they know in order to enter into ministry. Everybody is called to lead a missional life, and living missionally can happen wherever we are, no matter where we have come from or what we are doing. We are created to live fully, and in order to do so, in order to live missionally, all we need to do is fully own who we are. We need to become the people God created us to be, bearers of God's image called to live lives worthy of the calling, filled with God's meaning, purpose, and hope.

Living Fully

In John 10:10, Jesus tells his disciples that the only reason he came to join us on this earth is in the hope that we could have life and have it abundantly. God desires for all of creation to live fully, to lead lives filled with abundant life, and this book is intended to help you find that fulfillment. This book is written in the hope that you might grab hold of some practical tools for uncovering true meaning and purpose in all that you do.

Regardless of where you are or what you're doing, this book is intended to give you the tools and ability to live fully, to live with mission and purpose so that you can experience all that God has in store for you as one who bears God's image in the world. This book is about pursuing God. This book is about living fully in search of God's presence that you might have life and have it abundantly.

• • •

I want you to imagine a young attorney who is living in an urban center. His life is fixed on the idea of becoming high-powered and successful. He dreams of driving a black Mercedes, living in a loft decorated with furniture from Crate and Barrel, and always having the latest technological gadgets in hand. Can you picture him?

After taking the right courses and earning the right grades, he gets accepted into the right schools. Those schools enable him to get the right clerkship, which allows him to land the right job with a generous signing bonus. By the time

Is this you?

he turns twenty-eight, he's labeled a rising expert in the law, and his future is bright and beautiful.

Can you picture him?

My guess is that you probably know some individuals like this. Maybe they aren't attorneys. Maybe they are bankers or consultants or doctors or some other professional types. Maybe they aren't any of these things.

Maybe this is you. Or maybe you want this to be you.

In Luke 10:25, we meet a person just like this. He's a young attorney, an expert in the Law. This person walks up to Jesus and asks him, "Teacher, . . . what must I do to inherit eternal life?"

How could this be? How could a person who has made all the right decisions, has attended all the right schools, has landed all the right internships, and is now working the best job still ask a question like this? How is it possible that he still wants more when he seems to have it all already?

"Jesus," he relates, "I've done all the right things. I've done everything I was supposed to, but something still seems to be missing. Jesus, what must I do to find it? What must I do to have life?" And there it is—the million-dollar question. "What must I do to have life? What must I do to live fully, to live with purpose, to live a life that matters? What must I do to inherit eternal life?"

• • •

No matter how old or young we are, no matter how successful or unsuccessful we might be, one thing is certain: we all wrestle with questions of purpose. We desire meaning. We long to find fulfillment, and so most of us wander through life pursuing answers to the following questions:

Who am I?

Why am I here?

What am I supposed to do with my life?

These are the substantive questions that drive every-thing we do. These are the questions that frame our decisions about work, school, family, friends, where we live, what we buy, and ultimately what we choose to do or not do with our lives.

As a pastor working in downtown Kansas City, I encoun-ter these questions everywhere I turn. A vast majority of the professional men and women I meet with (both young and old) feel as though they aren't really *living*. They are trudging. They are slogging through life, existing and wrestling in the hopes that they might eventually find fulfillment, meaning, and purpose. Instead of *living*, these professional men and women spend seventy to eighty hours a week earning, spend-ing, and accumulating material possessions in the hope that they might find life in wealth.

We work hard in search of the good life. Society encour-ages it. Unfortunately when we don't find what we're looking for at work, we begin to play hard in the hope that we might find it in various diversions. When we come up empty in those diversions, we eventually find ourselves in all of our efforts, in work and in play, feeling more and more trapped and less and less hopeful.

From childhood we are trained to work hard, to travel down pathways that we believe will help us succeed and thrive in life. These are the pathways that afford us the opportunity and resources to change the world initially, yet somehow they end up robbing us of the very thing we wanted all along. Instead of living our dreams we end up living small, empty lives that look similar to each other.

I spend time with men and women who share stories like this on a regular basis. They have all worked hard to land a job that offered a great sense of meaning and purpose, but somewhere down the line, they've lost any hope of ever finding the fulfillment they were searching for. So we meet for coffee in the middle of their busy workweek, and they ask me, "What must I do in order to live fully?"

Have you ever asked this question?

Have you ever felt as though you weren't getting the most out of life?

• • •

I found myself sitting at a restaurant in Kansas City not too long ago with a guy named Joe. Joe was a rising star. Joe's company was investing in him. He said, "They are grooming me and positioning me in order that I might one day become the dynamic leader they need to take this company to the next level."

I had originally come to know Joe because we were neighbors living in the same downtown high-rise. However, our interactions had been limited to small talk. One day Joe elevated the conversation and asked me if I'd be up for having lunch sometime. I said, "Sure."

So there we were sitting at lunch, and I felt like an honored guest. (After all, he was a rising star!) We made it about halfway through our salads when the conversation turned more serious. He said, "Scott, the reason I invited you out to lunch today is because every time I see you or your wife, whether you're walking your dog or walking to your car,

I think to myself, 'I wish I had the sense of purpose you have.' You see, when someone told me that you were both pastors, I couldn't help but think that what you have is the very thing I'm missing. I feel empty. I feel like I'm missing something. I feel like I have this gaping hole in my life, and that no matter how much I stuff in it, I can't fill it up."

Wow! I thought. *How could this be? On the surface, he had everything.*

All I could say in reply was, "Joe, I'm shocked!"

On the outside, Joe was a successful individual. He was an accomplished professional, living a very healthy life. He was married and fit. He and his wife owned a great home. He had a well-paying, challenging job, and he and his wife were even expecting their first child. Yet something was missing: He wasn't happy, wasn't fulfilled, and didn't have that sense of being whole.

And that's when he got very direct with me.

"Scott, I think about my life and I know I have a lot of great things going on, but I would trade all of it to understand why I'm here. I don't know why I'm doing the things I'm doing. I feel like I have so much to offer, but I don't know what to do. I don't have a purpose, a calling, or a mission."

This feeling of misdirection or emptiness is not exclusive to those who seem to have it all. It applies to nearly everyone I come into contact with as a pastor serving an urban area. They all have wondered—to what end am I doing this, anyway?

In the Western world, we have so many of the material comforts that we desire. Even if we don't, we at least have the nonmaterial blessings of happy friends and family; and yet still we lead lives of quiet desperation, understanding nothing but the fact that there is an emptiness plaguing us. No matter how much we try, no matter how much food, technology, or exercise we pour into it, no matter how many iPads and wristwatches we stuff it with, no matter how many children, partners, and friends we parade around the edges of it, it still plagues us. We need something more.

Over time, our inability to fill that hole and to answer that question takes its toll on us. It gets to the point for some that not knowing what we're here to do actually creates an internal ache. For others, it looks like depression. For others still, it looks like monotony, repetition, or meaninglessness. Whatever description we might apply to it, not knowing why we are here on earth feels like an illness or a disease: it plagues us wherever we go.

My friend Joe, like the young attorney in Luke, and like so many other people, was lacking purpose, and it was plaguing him. He didn't know how to live fully.

● ● ●

The good news is that the God of the universe has a restorative purpose for your life. Jeremiah 29:11 reads, "'For I know the plans I have for you,' declares the LORD, 'plans to prosper you and not to harm you, plans to give you hope and a future.'" In John 10:10, Jesus explains to his disciples and us that we are to have life and have it abundantly. Jesus tells his disciples, "The thief comes only to steal and kill and destroy; I have come that they may have life, and have it to the full." How incredible is that?

If you look at this passage of Scripture from a different angle, Jesus tells us that his desire is for us to live fully and completely with a sense of personal mission and peace.

But some substantive questions still remain.

What does this look like?

How can we live fully? Or, how can we lead a missional life?

• • •

In Luke 10:26-28, Jesus answers the young attorney by asking him to recite what Scripture says about abundant life. The legal expert responds to Jesus saying, "That's easy! You shall love the Lord your God with all your heart, and with all your soul, and with all your strength, and with all your mind, and love your neighbor as yourself" (paraphrased).

Jesus smiles and tells him, "You have given the right answer; now do this, and you will fully live" (paraphrased).

Living fully isn't an activity. It doesn't consist of a set of specific practices. It's a way of viewing the world in its many dimensions and finding the courage to live into it. Missional living is seeing the world and everything in it as a gift and opportunity to meet and experience God's perfect love and then sharing that love with everyone we meet, in every situation, in all we do. We have the ability to transform our lives according to God's gifts.

Jesus came to the earth so that we might all have the ability to live fully. Living fully is nothing more than loving God with everything we have and then learning how to love our neighbors in the same way. It requires all that we are and all that we have. It requires our whole being.

Over the course of history, God's mission for all of creation (*missio Dei*) has been thoroughly debated. Scholars have thousands of ways of understanding it and talking about it. Of the more accepted interpretations, some say that God came to reconcile the nations, to bring people of all nations together as one. Others say that God came to seek and save those who

COMMUNION

were lost, meaning that God came specifically (and especially) for those who didn't know him, who couldn't see him, or didn't believe in him. He came for the stranger, the oppressed, the sinful, and skeptical. Still others say that God's mission is to redeem and restore all of creation, meaning that God's desire is that all things, both seen and unseen, will one day come together perfectly to reflect the full image of God and in the process create a new heaven and a new earth.

Communion

I've always believed God's mission is best reflected in a picture of perfect communion (we'll unpack this in a few paragraphs). God desires for us to become one with each other and one with him, that we might all be one in ministry to all the world—in other words, that we might live in perfect communion. This is what Jesus tells the young attorney in Luke 10 when he says, "You shall love God with everything you have, and love your neighbor in the same way" (paraphrased). This is ultimately what Jesus modeled for all of creation throughout his life, especially on the night he gave himself up for the world.

Rather than hiding, fighting, running, or resisting the Romans, Jesus, in his last days, sought to gather his closest friends together in community. To celebrate his very last night on earth, Jesus and his disciples shared a meal. Little did we know that hidden among his friends were people who would betray him, forsake him, and abandon him in his moment of greatest need. Nevertheless, rather than taking care of himself, Jesus gathered his twelve disciples together that they might share in one last supper, so they could eat bread and drink wine. That night they experienced Holy Communion.

25

"Communion" is derived from the Latin word *commu-nion*, meaning "to share in common." Its corresponding term in Greek is translated as "fellowship" or "community." For many Christians, the basic meaning of "communion" points us to an especially close relationship shared between individuals or between a community of faith and God. I believe this is exactly what God desires. I believe this is God's mission.

God desires for us to become closely connected. This happens when we strive to live life in harmony with each other, with God, and in ministry to all the world. This is perfect communion. This is God's mission. It is oneness. It is the perfect love of God and neighbor. It is living in a way that demonstrates love toward God and that cares for those around us in the same way we care for ourselves. This is what happens whenever we gather around a table to share a meal. This happens whenever communities of faith gather together as strangers and as friends in order to eat, drink, and remember the mighty and selfless acts of Jesus Christ. God's mission is perfect communion, and so God desires for us to live our lives in the hope that we might see everything we do as an opportunity to grow closer to each other and to grow closer to God in love. On Good Friday, this becomes our mission.

In Matthew 27, Christ was betrayed, condemned, crucified, and left for dead. As Jesus hung on the cross, "The carpenter's son cried with a loud voice and breathed his last." At that very moment, the curtain hanging in the temple was torn in two. It ripped from top to bottom.

Initially, this might seem like an insignificant event. Curtains rip all the time. This curtain, however, was the only physical thing separating humanity from God. It separated the flesh from the divine. This curtain was the veil that draped the holy of holies (the heart of God). It obstructed us from becoming one with God, from loving him and from entering into the heart of God. Yet Scripture tells us that as Jesus breathed his last, it was this fabric, the temple curtain, the only remaining symbol preventing us from living fully, that had been torn. At that moment, we were given the greatest gift of all time. We were given meaning, purpose, and hope. We were blessed with the ability (for the first time since Adam and Eve in Genesis) to become one with God and one with each other in perfect love. On Good Friday the curtain tore in two, our mission became God's mission, and perfect communion was possible once again.

Through Jesus' life, death, and resurrection, the barriers between God and humanity were removed. The temple curtain was torn in two, and we were freed by the grace of Jesus Christ to live fully as the people we were created to be. We are people made in God's image. Our purpose is to love God with everything we have and to do the same for our neighbors. In Matthew 27, Jesus made it possible for us to experience God fully.

After Good Friday, one of the greatest mysteries of the Christian faith is that we no longer need to come to a temple or other holy place to meet God. We can now encounter God and discover his mission wherever we are, just as we are. It is our pursuit of God in all of life's dimensions that constitutes the bedrock of the missional life.

Seven Dimensions of a Missional Life

The missional life is a life oriented toward God. It is a life rooted in the pursuit of God's presence everywhere, in everything, and in everyone. As I think of the missional life, I've come to discover seven dimensions that seem to give our lives great shape and richness. You might be asking, "Why seven?" I believe there are seven because the number seven seems to be biblical. From the seven days of creation in Genesis to the seven churches in Revelation, the number seven most often represents the fullness of God's creation. On the seventh day, God finished his labor, rested, and enjoyed this wonderful creation. As Moses and the Israelites wandered through the wilderness escaping Egyptian slavery, God delivered to them manna, or the bread of heaven. This edible gift fell from the sky in a seven-day cycle. Peter asked Jesus how often he should forgive. Specifically, Peter asked whether seven times was enough. Jesus responded, "Not seven times, but seventy-seven times" (Matthew 18:22). In his final day, Jesus offered seven last words.

I believe that seven is a numerical representation of perfection, of fullness or abundance. However, I arrived at seven dimensions because that is the number of dimensions upon which I have centered my life in my own attempt to live fully. As I have sought to live missionally in my own life, I have discovered abundant life. Incidentally, these are also the dimensions that have served as the foundation for our growing Christian community in downtown Kansas City.

Falling on Our Knees

I believe the missional life begins with worship. Worship helps us understand who God is, who we are, and what we're called to do. Worship helps us know who we were created to be and instructs us in how to go about becoming those people. Through worship we discover that the missional life is less about leading and more about following. It is less about climbing ladders and more about falling on our knees. Living fully, or missionally, requires that we empty ourselves of all our expectations and rid ourselves of the notion that we are God in order that we might be filled with new life, a new Spirit, and a renewed desire to live and see the world differently. Worship shapes our vision that we might see this world as something other than our own. It helps us remember that God is God and we are not. More than anything else, worship helps us know how to love God with everything we have—with our heart, mind, strength, and spirit.

Reading Scripture

Living missionally also requires that we strive to grow in the knowledge and understanding of God. The missional life is rooted in God's perfect love but also requires our minds. Living fully is about the heart, but it also demands that we grow in knowledge and understanding. In order to continue growing in both knowledge and love, it is important that we spend time reading Scripture, learning the story, and remembering God's love for us.

Living fully means resisting the urge to check our brains at the door. More than anything, God desires all of us, which includes our insight, our questions, and our reasoning. In order to employ these gifts, we must continue to seek truth and meaning. Central to this is the study of Scripture. Missional living requires that we immerse ourselves in Scripture, not for personal intellectual ascent or for the glory of reciting passages on the spot, but because we are called to love God with everything we have. We must read Scripture in order to learn who God is, to remember God's mission, and to place our story into God's larger story. We should aim to fall in love with the Word of God in order to fall in love with God all over again and be transformed in such a way that our lives are filled with renewed purpose.

Making Friends Out of Strangers

Living fully continues as we learn how to love our neighbors as ourselves, which mandates making friends out of strangers. Missional living involves building community, making friends, and transforming the world by loving our neighbors as ourselves. This happens one person at a time. In an age of increasing technology and in a culture that values connectivity over presence, living fully demands that we pursue opportunities to physically gather together and spend time with each other, to serve one another, and to remember who we are no matter where we are or what we are going through. If the missional life requires that we view and pursue every encounter we have with others as an opportunity to become one with each other, then living fully happens when we reach out, invite, and make friends out of strangers.

Breaking Bread

Throughout history, God has used bread to connect with his people. From Exodus to Ezekiel and from the Sea of Galilee to the Upper Room, bread has been present. Even after Jesus died and rose again, God met his disciples in the breaking of bread on the road to Emmaus. We have the opportunity to meet God whenever we break bread together. In the church we call the breaking of bread Holy Communion. This can be a very confusing practice, yet at the same time it is central to defining God's mission, who we are, and what we were created to be.

However, the missional life is not about the food. It is not about feeding a physical hunger with a simple snack. It is about meeting God and experiencing the full depth of companionship or friendship both with God and one another. Breaking bread together is about being filled to overflowing with the perfect love of God and neighbor and then seeing every table you sit at as an opportunity to invite others to experience the same thing.

Praying Always

In order to live fully we must also be willing to pray. When most of us think about prayer, we think about and treat God and prayer in a similar fashion. Prayer for many people looks like asking God for the things we want, when we want them; then when we get them, we find fulfillment, meaning, and purpose. Is that really what prayer is? And is that really how God works? Is living a missional life dependent upon a God who serves as a genie for adults?

James would disagree. He writes,

Is anyone among you in trouble? Let them pray. Is anyone happy? Let them sing songs of praise. Is anyone among you sick? Let them call the elders of the church to pray over them and anoint them with oil in the name of the Lord. And the prayer offered in faith will make the sick person well; the Lord will raise them up. If they have sinned, they will be forgiven. Therefore confess your sins to each other and pray for each other so that you may be healed. The prayer of a righteous person is powerful and effective. (James 5:13-16)

Prayer helps us live fully but not in the ways we might expect. When we pray, we root ourselves in holy conversation.

We experience an ongoing dialogue, where God's voice and God's presence can be pursued and discovered everywhere we turn.

Spending Less and Giving More

Jesus tells his disciples, "You cannot serve both God and money" (Matthew 6:24). The apostle Paul writes to Timothy assuring him that "the love of money is a root of all kinds of evil. Some people, eager for money, have wandered from the faith and pierced themselves with many griefs" (1 Timothy 6:10). Additionally, the book of Proverbs continually references the virtue of generosity. Therefore, living fully requires that we learn how to spend less and give more of what God has given to us.

Body Building

Our bodies are gifts from God. Therefore we must learn how to lift weights. They are the lodging place for the love of God or the Holy Spirit's dwelling place. In creation, God forms us from the dust of the earth and then breathes life into us. He created us in God's image, and that is very good!

Over the last two years I have discovered the importance of caring for my body, the most amazing gift I have been given. When we take care of our bodies, eat well, and stay in shape, our lives will better reveal the glory of God. This will forever allow us to view the world with better clarity and insight. Understanding our lives, and specifically our bodies, as gifts given to us will ultimately lead us directly into God's beating heart.

Living Fully: Singing, Painting, Laughing, and Dancing

Living fully requires that we enjoy life. The missional life is learning how to see God everywhere we turn.

Living a missional life requires that we search for God in all things and that we live into the heart of God by embracing and enjoying a spirit of creativity and joyful expression. We were created in the image of God, and therefore, we were made to reflect the beautiful and diverse image of our creator God. Therefore, living fully is rooted in searching for God's image in everything that has breath.

These are what I have come to know as the seven dimensions to the missional life. Living fully requires that we give everything we have, our whole lives, so that our heads, hearts, and hands might grab hold of God's goodness and mercy, which abound throughout all of creation and satisfy the deepest longings of the human heart. The God of the universe, who created all things and in whom all creatures live, move, and have their being, has a mission for us. By the grace of Jesus Christ we are invited to live fully into this mission.

When we focus our time and energy on these seven dimensions of what I would call the missional life, then and only then can we fully live. Then and only then can we become the people we were created to be!

Altering Our Vision

"A Christian leader is not a leader because he announces a new idea and tries to convince others of its worth; he is a leader because he faces the world with eyes full of expectation, with the expertise to take away the veil that covers its hidden potential."
—Henri Nouwen, *The Wounded Healer*

I have had a fascination with Superman for as long as I can remember. When I was little—maybe five or six—my mother made me a Superman cape. Superman was my hero. So I wore that Superman cape wherever I traveled. I watched all of the Superman movies. I had all of the Superman action figures. I had one of those old-school Superman punching dummies. I ate Superman ice cream. I wore Superman underwear. As if that wasn't enough, I carried my Superman obsession out of my adolescence and into the nineties. I, like most people, had become addicted to *Seinfeld*. It didn't take long to realize that the writers of *Seinfeld* loved Superman as much as I did. (Did you know that there isn't a *Seinfeld* episode where you do not see the man of steel?)

The simple fact is this: I loved Superman and still do, but for the life of me I could not and cannot understand why nobody at the *Daily Planet*, the newspaper where Clark Kent worked, ever recognized that Clark Kent was Superman.

It was so obvious to me. So what was it about everyone working there (or everybody living in Metropolis for that matter) that they couldn't see Clark Kent for who he really was?

Were his glasses really that distracting? Was his haircut that different?

I don't think so.

Over the past few years, I've realized that there was something wrong with the people at the *Daily Planet*, and there's something wrong with many of us. Together we struggle to see things for what they really are. The missional life first and foremost is about looking at things differently. It's about seeing things for what they really are. It's about looking, seeing, and searching for the presence of God wherever we are and wherever we go.

And this is difficult to do. It always has been, and it always will be. We are too easily distracted by our work, by our own experience, and by our need to be in control.

In Mark 6, Jesus was about thirty years old. He had just returned home to Nazareth for the first time since he began healing the masses, exorcising demons, calming storms, and foretelling the coming kingdom. He had been doing amazing things that only God could do. After a series of miracles and life-changing ministry, Jesus returned to his hometown hoping to find some comfort, familiar faces, and maybe a few pats on the back.

Instead he discovered that nobody cared about his ability to perform miracles. They didn't notice anything different about him at all. They couldn't see him for who he really was.

All of these amazing things had been happening in and around Galilee. Jesus had been changing the world, healing the sick, and feeding the hungry, but nobody took notice. Until Jesus began to preach. Once he started to speak, the people in Nazareth took offense at Jesus' bold claims of power and authority. Mark writes,

> Jesus left there and went to his hometown, accompanied by his disciples. When the Sabbath came, he began to teach in the synagogue, and many who heard him were amazed. "Where did this man get these things?" they asked. "What's this wisdom that has been given him? What are these remarkable miracles he is performing? Isn't this the carpenter? Isn't this Mary's son and the brother of James, Joseph, Judas and Simon? Aren't his sisters here with us?" And they took offense at him. (6:1-3)

These people were working at the *Daily Planet*. They could not see Superman even though he was right there: they

SUPERMAN

could see only Clark Kent. Jesus is the Son of God, and he was standing before them, but all they saw was the son of a carpenter. They saw the guy who had built doors, crafted tables, made chairs, and repaired furniture. He was the guy who visited their homes, called on their businesses, and worked for a price. He was anything but extraordinary. He was just Jesus from Nazareth, Mary's boy, nothing more. What's worse was that these townspeople had heard about the healings. They knew of his growing popularity and had even witnessed a few of Jesus' miracles, but they still didn't believe.

This is what happens when we are unwilling to see past our own experience. This is what happens when we stop searching for deeper meaning and purpose. This is what happens when we stop searching for God or, worse yet, never start.

The townspeople of Nazareth didn't recognize Jesus for who he really was because they weren't looking for God. To think that Jesus might be who he said he was was unfathomable. It was heresy. In their minds, carpenters couldn't change the world. Woodworkers didn't possess lifesaving or life-giving power. In their world, the regular people didn't possess the power to heal people, perform miracles, or do God's work. Even though the Son of God was standing before them, they couldn't see him for who he was. They couldn't see Superman.

Vision Problems

In Luke 10 we meet up with a pair of sisters, Mary and Martha, one of whom has trouble seeing. Mary and Martha's story begins in verse 38:

> Now as they went on their way, he entered a certain village, where a woman named Martha welcomed him into her home. She had a sister named Mary, who sat at

the Lord's feet and listened to what he was saying. But Martha was distracted by her many tasks; so she came to him and asked, "Lord, do you not care that my sister has left me to do all the work by myself? Tell her then to help me." But the Lord answered her, "Martha, Martha, you are worried and distracted by many things; there is need of only one thing. Mary has chosen the better part, which will not be taken away from her." (vv. 38-42, NRSV)

In this story Mary and Martha both welcome Jesus into their home, but things change once he enters. The moment Jesus crosses the threshold, Mary and Martha respond to his presence differently. Mary spends all of her time sitting at Jesus' feet listening to every word he has to say. Martha, on the other hand, spends all of her time working frantically. Scripture describes her as being "distracted by her many tasks."

Having so much to do with so little help, Martha approaches Jesus and in effect asks him, "Why aren't you commanding Mary to help me out?"

Jesus replies by saying, "Mary has chosen the better part."

The *New Living Translation* puts it this way, Jesus says, "There is only one thing worth being concerned about. Mary has discovered it, and it will not be taken away from her" (vv. 41-42, NLT).

In this story Jesus tells Martha that Mary was able to see something that she couldn't. Mary could see Superman, while Martha was simply working at the *Daily Planet*. Mary could see the Son of God, while Martha could only see the work before her. It is interesting to note that Mary's vision enabled her to eventually be the one who anoints Jesus as Messiah with the costly perfume and then wipes his feet with her hair before Jesus heads into Holy Week.

In order to live fully, in order to catch a glimpse of the glory of the coming of the Lord, we must be willing, like Mary, to strip it all away—to stop our work in order that we might see and pursue God everywhere we go.

Whether it's Metropolis and Superman, the Jews and Jesus, or Mary and Martha, we have trouble seeing things for what they really are. We have a vision problem.

How's your eyesight doing these days?

The missional life is about refocusing our eyes. It's about altering the way we see things. It's about searching for glimpses of God, even in the most unexpected places and unlikely faces. It's looking for God's presence everywhere we go.

Generally speaking, we see people, places, and pathways according to what we want to see. High school reunions are perfect examples of this. What would happen if you were to go back to your high school reunion today? What would you see?

Regardless of your answer, my guess is that there are former classmates who would gasp upon seeing you now, five, ten, or fifteen years later. They would say things like, "You're doing what? Really?" They'd launch into those wonderful "I remember when" stories. They'd see you, not as the person you are now, but as the person you were then.

We do these kinds of things because we have a hard time seeing the world around us as anything other than what we know, and based on that limited worldview we say things like, "People don't change. You are who you are, and nothing will ever change that." In the same way, the folks in Nazareth cried out, "Jesus isn't the son of God; he's a carpenter." Lois Lane said, "Clark Kent can't be Superman because he works at the *Daily Planet.*"

We struggle to see the big picture. We struggle to find God's life-giving presence and power even though it is all around us. We say, "Our high school friends can't be doctors, lawyers, or bankers because they'll always be our high school friends!" We believe that we cannot do anything of worth if we stay at this company, in this position, or in this city. We struggle to remember that the world isn't ours. "The earth is [God's], and everything in it," sings the psalmist (Psalm 24:1).

Our vision problem, our shortsightedness, and our inability to see everything around us as a gift and an opportunity for transformation prevents us from seeing and meeting the living God, Creator of the universe. It prevents us from experiencing and sharing God's life-giving and lifesaving work. It prevents us from living fully, but it doesn't have to.

In John 11, we meet a guy named Lazarus. We quickly discover that Lazarus is very sick. In fact, Lazarus is dying. At first glance, you might not know who Lazarus is, but I'm certain you remember his sisters, Mary and Martha. In John 11 we discover that Mary and Martha are grieving his illness and impending death. So Mary and Martha take action and call for Jesus, and Jesus comes running.

When Jesus arrives, he discovers that Lazarus has already been in the tomb for four days. When Martha hears that Jesus is coming, she goes to meet him, while Mary stays home. Upon meeting Jesus on the road to Bethany, Martha says to Jesus, "Lord, . . . if you had been here, my brother would not have died. But I know that even now God will give you whatever you ask" (vv. 21-22).

How's your eyesight
these days?

What I love about this story is that Martha finally sees. She is redeemed. In this story, it's Martha, not Mary, who approaches Jesus. It is Martha, not Mary, who sees Jesus as the one who has the power over death. The woman who had previously been too busy to see Superman finally begins to see Jesus for who he really is, and what happens as a result is absolutely remarkable.

In the midst of her grief she says, "Lord, if you had been here earlier, my brother would not have died. But even now (even though he's been dead for four days already) I know that you have the power to heal him."

In the face of Lazarus's death, Martha's confidence is undiminished. In fact, her confidence is increased; and that is exactly what it means to live fully. That is the definition of faith. That is the conviction of things unseen, the assurance of things hoped for (see Hebrews 11:1). This is what happens next.

Upon hearing Martha's confession and being moved by her faith, Jesus replies by assuring her of all the things she hoped for, her unseen convictions. He tells her, "'Your brother will rise again. . . . I am the resurrection and the life. Those who believe in me, even though they die, will live, and everyone who lives and believes in me will never die. Do you believe this?' She said to him, 'Yes, Lord, I believe that you are the Messiah, the Son of God, the one coming into the world'" (John 11:23, 25-27, NRSV).

Then Jesus goes to the tomb where Lazarus was buried. He rolls away the stone and cries with a loud voice, "Lazarus, come out!" (v. 43).

Lazarus comes out. He is unbound, resurrected, and set free. What once was lost has now been found. What has once

been dead, buried, and abandoned for four whole days has
been brought back to life. And it all happens after Martha—
the one who had previously been unable to see God, the one
who hasn't ever stopped to recognize Jesus—finally sees Jesus
for who he really is. She slows down long enough to peer be-
neath the surface, and when she does she sees Superman. She
sees Jesus, the Resurrection and the Life.

Are you seeing things clearly these days? Or are you
working at the *Daily Planet*?

Are you slowing down to search for and pursue God? Or
are you distracted by your many tasks?

In John 11, Jesus raises to the newness of life a man who
had been dead for four days. This is what can happen when
we focus our eyes on the things that are not broadly seen. Life
abounds when we're willing to strip away the veneer and see
things for what they really are. When we search for and pursue
God, our lives are undoubtedly changed, as finally we are able
to experience the fullness of God's presence and power.

The missional life is about altering our vision. It demands
that we adjust our vision to the divine rhythms of the God in
whom and through whom we "live and move and have our
being" (Acts 17:28). It's about shifting the way we see things.
Pursuing God requires that we look for evidence of God's presence wherever we are and wherever we go, and let me assure you
that God is working everywhere. God's presence, God's surprising and transforming power, even lives in you.

God is in all things and through all things. God's love
"bears all things, believes all things, hopes all things, and
endures all things" (1 Corinthians 13:7, NRSV). What's more
is that God calls us through all kinds of mediums (vocations,
locations, personalities, and talents) to join in God's mission

of perfect love of God and neighbor—or holy communion. Living missionally allows us to encounter and experience the transformative power and presence of the living God in a way that draws us (and those around us) into loving relationship or perfect communion.

Let's Start with Confession

Living fully requires that we recognize our "fleshy" propensity to see Clark Kent when we're really looking at Superman. We must get past our tendency to write off, rebuke, and rebuff others when they speak words, hold beliefs, or live in ways that we disagree with or cannot imagine. We must acknowledge and confess that we don't see things such as our jobs, normal encounters, or daily interactions for what they really are—opportunities to participate in the lifesaving and world-changing work of God—but rather as ways to outperform our neighbors, friends, competitors, and coworkers.

Living fully begins with confession. The missional life requires that we acknowledge or confess our shortsightedness (our problem) in order that we might live into and enjoy God's world. It demands that we open our eyes in a way that unclasps the unexpected power and presence of the living God in order to live fully with meaning, purpose, and hope. This begins with confession and takes shape through God's forgiveness or through the grace of Jesus Christ.

I don't normally sing, but I enjoy good music. In the early church, and especially in the earliest days of the Methodist movement, hymns were a primary avenue for teaching people about who God is and how God works in the world. Some hymns were also sung as prayers. As we sing, so we pray. In 1895, Clara Scott wrote the words to a traditional hymn.

These words seem to convey the heart of the missional life better than any book or lecture might.

The missional life is rooted in our ability to live lives that pray and hope for the following:

> *Open my eyes, that I may see*
> *Glimpses of truth Thou hast for me;*
> *Place in my hands the wonderful key*
> *That shall unclasp and set me free.*

> *Silently now I wait for Thee,*
> *Ready, my God, Thy will to see.*
> *Open my eyes, illumine me,*
> *Spirit divine.*

Although I've admittedly always had a fascination with Superman, somewhere along the way I came to the realization that I am not a superhero. I am just Scott. I always have been and always will be. I am Sue and Dave's son. I am Karin and Jill's brother. I am Wendy's husband. I am a former investment analyst, a graduate of Duke Divinity School. I am a guy who gets overly competitive playing on the soccer field, a guy who loves baseball, and a guy who likes to laugh out loud a lot. I'm not all that impressive on the outside. Inside, however, I know that God has plans for me. My mission is to simply live in a way that searches for the glimpses of truth that God has for me in every encounter, in everything I see and do, to the end that I meet God and join in his life-giving and lifesaving mission of holy communion (the perfect love of God and neighbor). If I do this, then I might find abundant life.

My prayer is that somehow by the grace of God you might realize that God has plans for you as well. No matter where you are or what you are doing, where you have come

Illumine

from or where you are going in the future, my prayer is that you might discover that you have the ability to live fully here and now. My hope is that you will discover that the image of God is alive in you and that you too are meant to have life and have it abundantly.

My hope is that this book will help you in your own personal pursuit of meaning and purpose. I pray that it will help you commit to a new way of life that sees all things as opportunities to become entangled in God's mission in the world.

Falling on Our Knees

"I don't know where you've been or what you've done. My hope is that every time you walk into this place you will meet God. I expect that somehow through the singing of songs, through the reading of Scripture, through the preaching of the living word, you will have an encounter with the living God. I expect you to meet God here today."

—Resurrection Downtown

Worship is something we do. It shapes who we are. It orients our worldview, and it opens our lives to the leading and prompting of the Holy Spirit, or the presence of God all around us. Worship is first and foremost about meeting God.

Worship is a place where we encounter God in a way that brings us to our knees. We are made low in worship because God is that big!

When is the last time you attended a worship service?

What did you expect to happen when you attended that worship service?

I hope you were expecting something.

Wherever we are and wherever we go in this world, we are met with expectations. From the moment we were born, most of our parents began expecting that we would grow up to achieve great things. Mothers and fathers dream of college scholarships, public office appointments, charitable service, brilliant ideas, innovation, superior athletic ability, and a drive that will change the world. Our teachers expect that we'll pay attention in class, do our homework, and strive to earn good grades. Our coaches expect that we practice as hard as we play. Our employers expect that we will be sold out for the good of the organization. Our spouses expect us to know what they are thinking and feeling, and children expect that their parents actually know how to parent. Even our government officials expect that we'll serve our country faithfully and selflessly. Everyone expects something of us.

I'm no different. I have high expectations not only for my life but for others as well. In fact, each week as I lead worship in downtown Kansas City, I make a point to set expectations for our congregation. I say, "I expect that each and every one of you will meet God here in this place." When we worship, we should expect to encounter God in a very real and powerful way. Worship is where we meet God and that's why it is so important.

When was the last time you worshiped and felt as though you met God?

Isaiah, the Old Testament prophet of God, offers us a vision of worship. In the sixth chapter of Isaiah, he describes what happens in worship. He casts a vision of what worship should look like and how it should feel. In this vision, Isaiah sees God the way I hope you see him every time you worship.

The prophet of God writes,

I saw the Lord, high and exalted, seated on a throne; and the train of his robe filled the temple. Above him were seraphim, each with six wings: With two wings they covered their faces, with two they covered their feet, and with two they were flying. And they were calling to one another: "Holy, holy, holy is the LORD Almighty; the whole earth is full of his glory." At the sound of their voices the doorposts and thresholds shook and the temple was filled with smoke. "Woe to me!" I cried. "I am ruined! For I am a man of unclean lips, and I live among a people of unclean lips, and my eyes have seen the King, the LORD Almighty." (vv. 1-5)

This is such a powerful picture. Isaiah describes the presence of God as being so big that only the train of his robe could fit inside the temple. The voices of the angels could be heard so clearly and so powerfully that their simple song caused the foundations of the temple to tremble. The combined power of the angels and the song causes Isaiah to physically fall down. On his knees, he bows down in humble admonition and offers a powerful confession, "Woe to me!"

This is worship. Worship is falling to our knees because of the all-powerful and overwhelming presence of God.

Have you ever experienced that before?

Do you ever go to worship expecting an experience like that?

I hope so.

People come to church with different expectations. We come expecting to be fed, helped, forgiven, changed. But when was the last time that happened for you?

What if you came into worship expecting an experience like that every time?

You should.

Worship should change us. The ancient Greeks used the word *proskuneo* to describe worship. This literally means "to bow down." Worship should bring us to our knees. It should be an experience that causes our legs to buckle and bend every time we enter the sanctuary because the presence of God is so overwhelming.

When was the last time worship brought you to your knees?

My guess is that it hasn't. Or if it has, it was a long, long time ago.

Powerful worship helps us to see things differently. Through worship we gain necessary perspective. By falling to our knees, we are humbled in God's presence and as a result we remember that as much as we would like to be, God is God and we are not.

Worship humbles us. It affords us an opportunity to confess, repent, and express the true condition of our heart. Worship allows us the opportunity to cry out from our knees,

*"Woe to me," I cried.
"I am ruined."*

as Isaiah did the doxology, a song of praise. And the second we do, we can begin to live fully.

The psalmist sings, "Come, let us bow down in worship, let us kneel before the LORD our Maker; for he is our God and we are the people of his pasture, the flock under his care" (Psalm 95:6-7).

On our knees in worship, we sing with the psalmist. On our knees in worship we can see the world for what it really is and not for what we think it should be. Worship opens the eyes of our hearts and allows us to see that the world is no longer ours to conquer and control but ours to love, live in, and enjoy by the grace of God.

Bowing down at the presence of God in worship orients us because we are made low. We take on a posture of humility. It allows us to put our heads on straight, and it restores our relationship with God to its right order. Most importantly, though, worship reminds us that God, as Creator of the universe, is ever present and leading us toward this vision of perfect communion—a world where we are one with each other, one with God, and one in mission to all the world. All we must do is follow wherever God leads us.

The Sweater-Vest Mission

To be honest, I have always struggled with the idea of worship as bowing down and then following wherever God leads. I have always been known as a leader, not as a follower. As the saying goes, "I bow down to no man," and this has been the case from a very early age.

At the age of twelve I devised a plan that would get me to where I wanted to go, and I (as opposed to God) was more than capable of getting myself there. My "there" was Wall

Street. I wanted to make it to Wall Street. So at the age of twelve, I did what any good leader would do, and I went to work.

I'm a product of the eighties, and as I mentioned earlier, my role model was Alex P. Keaton from *Family Ties*. I was the middle school student who wore the sweater-vest and a necktie. I was the high school student who carried the *Wall Street Journal* under my arm. I even had a portrait of Ronald Reagan hanging in my bedroom.

I started working my first real job at the age of thirteen. I began as a clerk at a local grocery store. By the age of fifteen, I had moved from that grocery store to a record store. I moved from the record store to a large ticket-selling company until I began working for my first investment firm at the age of eighteen. I worked there until I turned twenty-one, graduated from the University of Michigan, and became a junior partner at a small financial planning firm. I knew where I wanted to go, I had purpose, and I had a mission, but bowing down and following God was not a part of my plan. Good leaders don't follow. They *lead*.

Even though I found success at an early age, I felt increasingly empty. I was surrounded by a number of people (family, friends, and clients), but I still felt alone. From the age of thirteen to twenty-two, I worked hard to get the "right" job. I founded a fraternity, Alpha Sigma Phi, built my own business, and graduated from a well-respected university. Without knowing it, however, I lost focus. I wasn't seeing clearly. I had a vision problem. I also had a problem with control. I felt that I was still in control of my life. I was God and God was not.

As I continued working, I could not see beyond my all-consuming ambition. My pursuit of wealth and power left me feeling empty and alone. By the age of twenty-two, I had reached the lowest point in my life. I was lost and didn't know how to find a better path. This is what happens when we forget that God is God and we are not. This is what happens whenever we think we are in control. All this began to change when I received a phone call from my sister that same summer.

Jill's Song

Jill is my younger sister. Growing up, she was always shy. She was the girl who sat on the sidelines of every sporting event my family played in. It didn't matter whether she was courtside at tennis matches, on the sidelines at soccer games, or in the pit at gymnastics meets. She always sat quietly and patiently, blending into the background as the enthusiastic parents and crowds cheered and jeered.

I love my younger sister more than anything. I remember a particular phone conversation Jill and I had when she was a freshman in high school. She had been selected to sing a solo in an all-school assembly. She said, "Scott, there are going to be over 2,600 parents, students, and faculty there, but it would mean the most to me if you could be there."

Jill had always been there for me at every major event in my life. This was the least I could do for her in return. "I'll be there," I replied without hesitation.

As promised, I showed up at my old high school gymnasium. It was packed just as she said it would be. The crowd was tense and expectant. My sister, at the age of fourteen, was the featured vocalist. I had never been so nervous for another person before in my life.

There was my little sister, who always blended in, waiting to take the stage in front of thousands of people.

I struggled and strained in my seat to see her. When I caught a glimpse, I could see my sister dressed in what seemed to resemble clothing from the fifties. She was wearing a bright pink poodle skirt, a pressed white blouse, saddle shoes, and a matching pink scarf. Primed for what I feared would be her embarrassment, Jill took the microphone, waited for the accompanist, took a deep breath, and before a silent crowd began to sing. I was hanging on for dear life, hoping the performance wouldn't be a source of embarrassment for years to come.

I don't think I will ever forget the sound of her voice. She was singing a fifties sock hop, but with confidence and clarity. It was beautiful.

Never have I heard a sound so pure and so right come out of another person (let alone my little sister). In a matter of moments, she captivated the crowd with her beautiful singing. Her voice, her fearless posture, and her confident smile enveloped my whole imagination. My sister had stunned us into an awesome wonder. To this day, I still can't explain it, but for an instant, my little sister appeared to me as what seemed to be a light shining in the darkness. Her presence was illuminating. Her song, much like the angels' voices in Isaiah, was causing the foundations of my life to tremble.

As she performed, I couldn't help but bow my head. I was so surprised and overwhelmed by her confident spirit. I became weak in the knees as I thought to myself, *I want to be filled with that kind of confidence, that kind of smile, and that kind of power.* I whispered, "God, I need what she has." Without

GOD, I NEED
WHAT SHE HAS.

knowing it, my sister's performance was helping me discover the missional life. Jill had introduced me to worship.

Listening to my sister singing, I encountered something much bigger than myself. I began to realize how little I was, and this experience initiated a journey of self-understanding. I was discovering who I was, *whose* I was, and what I was created to be. My sister's song helped me realize that God was real and that I was not him. God was God and I was not. This is worship.

In the days that followed, I felt compelled to talk with Jill about her performance. I called her and said, "Jill, I feel like I have missed out on getting to know you and the beautiful woman you have become over these past few years. Would you be willing to let your older brother take you out on a date?"

She agreed, and I took her out for a cup of coffee and some long overdue conversation. The first thing I asked her was, "Where did you get that voice, and when did you become the kind of person with the confidence to stand up and sing such a beautiful song in front of so many people?"

Jill told me, "That's simple, my faith. My pursuit of God has made me the person I am today, Scott. Everything I have, including my voice and poise, I have received from God. I believe that God wants more than anything for me to share it with everyone I meet, everywhere I go."

Clearly, at some point in her life, she had discovered what it meant to live fully. Jill knew that she belonged to God. She was sharing all she had received from God and all she was with everyone around her. She was loving God and loving her neighbors. She was leading a missional life. And she was able to do so because of her faith, because of her worship.

Worship empowers us to live a life that sees and acknowledges that God is God. When we come to this realization, we also begin to see that the world is not ours and that everything we see, touch, taste, and hear is actually a gift. Who we are—our life, our breath, our intelligence, our skills, our possessions—are not ours, but God's; he has gifted us with everything we have.

Worship is falling to our knees in thanks and praise for all that God has given us—seen and unseen. Upon acknowledging this, our first response should be to sing with confidence, that we might share all we are with everyone we meet in a way that draws us closer together with God and each other. Living missionally is living a life of worship, giving away everything we have in order that others might meet God, fall to their knees, see their life as a gift, and then go and do likewise.

When my sister told me about her faith, I heard her words but didn't understand them. My inner selfishness or controlling tendency prevented me from processing what she was saying. I needed something practical. I wanted a step-by-step process to recover confidence. I needed something to go and do: an assignment, a contract to enter into, a task, or a plan. So we finished our cups of coffee and went our separate ways, and I continued on as I previously had until she called me again, about a year later.

Pink Vans and Pilgrimage

"Scott," she said, "I really need your help."

"What is it?"

"I need you to drive our youth group to the beach at Stoney Creek Metropark for the afternoon."

Okay, I supposed I could do her a favor. "What's required?"

"All you have to do is give up some of your time to drive one of the church's fifteen-passenger vans filled with my friends to a Metropark about forty-five minutes away. When we get there, you can either sit and read a book for three hours or you can drive to a coffee shop and wait there until we're done. Then you'll have to drive us back."

"Okay," I agreed. "I'll see you at the church."

I can still remember pulling into the church parking lot. There were about fifty high school students waiting desperately to go to the beach. Instead of one fifteen-passenger van, there were three. This was going to be interesting. There were more kids than seats.

We split up. I was designated the driver of the "pink van," with seventeen students assigned to our fifteen-passenger van. As it turned out, my sister was not one of my passengers. She was too embarrassed to be in the van her older brother was driving. With that vote of confidence, I began my chauffeuring pilgrimage to the beach. Honestly, I was simply hoping to make it back alive. We were no more than a few miles away from the church when a feeling of terror began to take hold of me. I realized that this trip was going to be something I would never forget.

The students, filled with pent-up energy, quickly seized control of the radio, turning the volume up so high that I was having trouble concentrating on the road. Then they started yelling, as if daring the radio to challenge them. I kept looking in the rearview mirror. All signs indicated that they were having what appeared to be a great experience. I, on the other hand, was not.

By the time we actually made it onto the expressway, the students had gone from singing and screaming to an exercise on how to slam into each other in the backseats of a van while driving at high speeds. At this point, not only had I clearly lost control of the radio, but because of their "exercising" I was losing control of the van as well. The students were rocking the van from side to side as we barreled down the expressway. It was at this point that I actually started to lose my composure.

I am not all that emotional, but driving a van overflowing with teenage strangers, listening to bad music at deafening levels, traveling seventy miles an hour while rocking back and forth was enough to push me over the edge. I began to cry, and I mean *really* cry.

With both hands on the wheel and tears rolling down my face, I didn't know what was happening to me. I didn't know what I was doing or why I was there, and the whole situation wasn't making any sense. All I had wanted to do was help out my little sister, and she wasn't even in my van.

As I began to lose my composure, the youth pastor sitting beside me in the passenger seat happened to look over at me and see my tears. Alarmed to see me in tears and not knowing me at all, he asked me if I was okay. He was clearly nervous that the person driving this out-of-control van appeared to be out of control himself. I quickly assured him that I was fine, but I also told him that I didn't know what was wrong with me. Then I heard myself say, "This whole experience is overwhelming me. It's bringing me to my knees." Inside I knew exactly what was going on. My foundations were trembling once again. The youth pastor and I spoke for the next forty-five minutes. We talked about the meaning of life.

The pink van

We talked about finding purpose and fulfillment. We talked about God.

Though I'm certain the rest of the van ride was as chaotic as it was when we started out, for whatever reason I don't remember anything but that conversation. By the end of the trip, I remember telling the youth pastor that I might be in the right place at the right time for the very first time in my life. It was surprising.

I did not have a voice like my sister's. Neither did I have her confidence. The only thing I had was my time, and for the first time, I was giving it away . . . to a bunch of teenagers. In return I was being filled with something amazing, something fulfilling, something life giving. I was emptying myself and sharing my gifts. In the process, I was being filled with abundant life and God's perfect love.

As the van pulled into the parking lot at Stoney Creek Metropark, I told the youth pastor that I thought God might be calling me to be a pastor.

The youth pastor said, "Scott, when I heard you were helping us drive these vans today, before you even showed up at the church, I was thinking the same thing."

Looking back at that trip, I think that experience was the first time I truly worshiped. The surprising power and presence of God's spirit in that chaotic, uncomfortable van filled with blaring music and loud voices was enough to force me to a place where I was humbled, hunched over, and crying. I had bowed down, and for the first time in a long time I had a chance to cry out loud. I was giving away the only thing I had, and in return I was being filled with new life. As a result, I found courage. I found a new kind of confidence. In my weakness and through my tears, I actually said to another person, a complete stranger, "I don't know why I am here. I don't know what I am supposed to do with my life." In my own way, I was saying, "God is God and I am not." I realized that I was not in control.

I still don't know if Jill knew what she was doing when she asked me to help her out, but I do know that for the first time in a long time I was finally in the right place. I was supposed to be there in that van with those people because the presence of the Lord was somehow in that place. I met God for the very first time in that van, and my eyes have never been the same since.

Worship is something that can happen anywhere God is present. The psalmist says, "Praise God in his sanctuary; praise him in his mighty heavens" (Psalm 150:1). We are called to praise him in all places and spaces at all times with all types of people. Worship trains us how we should live—in a way that constantly seeks to acknowledge that God is God and we are not.

The missional life begins in worship, where we meet and experience God's overwhelming and powerful presence in a way that transforms our lives for the ultimate transformation of the world.

1. John Calvin once said that our hearts are idol factories, continually inventing and manufacturing idols moment to moment. Sit in silence and reflect. What are the idols your heart is prone to assemble?

2. It is freeing to recognize God's greatness and our smallness; in what areas of your life do you try to be God rather than worship him?

3. Because worship is communing with God, it is an end in and of itself. As Christians, why do we rush past this portion of our faith? How might you better take up residency in worship?

Reading Scripture

"The word of God for the people of God.
Thanks be to God."

After my church van experience I had received a taste of God's presence. I had been filled with a new kind of purpose and meaning. However, as is the case with people who experience God for the very first time, I did not know what to do next. I didn't know anything other than God was God, I was not, and that I needed more direction in order to continue my pursuit of God. I was beginning to build community. I was worshiping. I was participating in holy communion by striving to love God and neighbor to the best of my limited ability, but I still needed more.

God desires that we strive to grow in knowledge and understanding of his unsearchable depth and love. The apostle Paul wrote to the early church in Colossae pleading to God on their behalf. He said,

> We continually ask God to fill you with the knowledge of his will through all the wisdom and understanding that the Spirit gives, so that you may live a life worthy of the Lord and please him in every way: bearing fruit in every good work, growing in the knowledge of God. (Colossians 1:9-10)

Living missionally means that we seek to grow in the knowledge of God. Living missionally requires that we live with a faith that seeks deeper understanding of God's grace. Another dimension of the missional life resides in our ability to read, reason, and grow in the knowledge of God. This begins as we read Scripture, learn the story of God, and constantly train our minds by studying the text.

As I stated earlier, living in constant pursuit of God demands that we fight the urge to check our brains at the door. God desires our insight and questions and delights in our reasoning. In order to employ the gifts we've been given, we must continue to seek out truth and meaning. We must grow in the infinite knowledge and love of God. Central to this is studying Scripture.

I read Scripture not for personal intellectual ascent, the glory of reciting passages on the spot, or the ability to boast in my familiarity, but because I desire to know God. I want to meet God and be filled with God's love and mercy. I read Scripture in order to know who God is and to remember how God has acted and intervened throughout history. I want to become familiar with God's mission and to place my story inside God's larger story.

When people ask me for help discerning direction and guidance pertaining to their career, family, and life circumstances, I often ask them, "When is the last time you opened the Bible?"

Gold-Embossed Bibles

In her book *Amazing Grace*, Kathleen Norris tells the story about a man named Arlo. Arlo was an older, hardworking man. He was a salt-of-the-earth type from an Iowa farming town. One day Arlo was sitting down to eat dinner with some friends from town when, out of the blue, he began talking about his grandfather who was a deeply religious man. As Arlo talked, he shared specifically about the Bible his grandfather had given to his bride and him as a wedding present nearly fifty years earlier.

Arlo admired this Bible. "It looked to be very expensive," he said. It was bound in white leather with their names and the date of their wedding engraved in gold lettering on the cover. Arlo recalled, "It was so nice looking that I left it in its box, and then, like so many other things do, it eventually

PLUS
INTEREST

ended up in our bedroom closet." But for months afterward, every time we saw Grandpa, he would ask me how I liked that Bible. He asked for years, "Have you read your Bible yet? How are you enjoying your Bible?" Arlo did not get it: he and his wife had written a thank-you note, and they'd even thanked him in person, but for some reason he wouldn't let it lie. He'd always ask about it.

After a tragedy led Arlo to do some housecleaning, he came across the Bible sitting on the floor in his bedroom closet. "Well," Arlo told his friends, "the second I opened up that Bible, the joke was on me. I finally took that Bible out of the closet and I found that Granddad had placed a twenty-dollar bill at the beginning of every book in the Bible—over $1,300 in all. All along he knew I wasn't reading!"

Together we laughed over this with Arlo as he began talking about the interest he could have made had he only found that money sooner. If only Arlo had known the true value of the gift contained in those pages! If only he had known the value of the love of Christ, waiting for him in that book.

In apostle Paul's letter to the Colossians, Paul writes to his church saying, "My goal is that they may be encouraged in heart and united in love, so that they may have the full riches of complete understanding, in order that they may know the mystery of God, namely, Christ" (2:2).

The true riches hiding inside the pages of Arlo's gold-embossed Bible far exceed $1,300 plus interest. The Bible contains "all the riches of assured understanding and . . . the knowledge of God's mystery" (2:2, NRSV).

In the Bible we can discover the gift of Christ himself, the most spectacular gift anyone could ever receive. But we have work to do to realize the gift of Christ and God's perfect love.

John Wesley, the founder of the Methodist movement, says that in order to experience this gift, in order to experience the love of Christ, we must wait by searching the Scriptures. Pursuing God means that we read Scripture daily. Like anything else, this requires time, the support of a community, and a desire to grow closer to God. Living fully becomes even more challenging when family, friends, and other obligations compete for our time and attention.

Do Not Worry About Your Life and Two Other Woes

I can still remember the day when I received my first grown-up Bible. I received it at a time when I was in the habit of reading John Grisham novels, *Sports Illustrated,* books on leadership, and basically anything that wasn't the Bible. When I opened the Bible for the very first time, I expected it to read as smoothly as a sports article covering the MVP of the Super Bowl. When I actually started reading it, I was severely disappointed by its hard-to-understand language, its endless genealogies, and its general inability to speak to where I was and the life I was looking for. I did not feel inspired or enriched, so I put it on my nightstand to rest. I figured I would read it when I really needed it.

In June of that same year, I began struggling with my diet. I could not eat anything without experiencing awful pains in my stomach. No matter what I did, and regardless of the doctor's orders, I could not shake shooting pains from plaguing my stomach. I tried a variety of different remedies, but nothing was able to soothe my pain. It was crippling and had been affecting me this way for about three months. One night, out of pure desperation, I picked up the Bible that was collecting dust on my nightstand and I opened it up.

When I opened it, the pages fell in such a way that my eyes landed immediately upon Matthew 6. Jesus said,

Therefore I tell you, do not worry about your life, what you will eat or drink; or about your body, what you will wear. Is not life more than food, and the body more than clothes? Look at the birds of the air; they do not sow or reap or store away in barns, and yet your heavenly Father feeds them. Are you not much more valuable than they? (6:25-26)

In that moment, I felt as though God was speaking to me directly. "Am I imagining this? Is this for real?" I thought. I was immediately calmed by what I read. A peace washed over me. I spent the next few nights reading and rereading that passage. Over time (after several weeks) I began feeling better. So, I closed my Bible back up.

Without pain and without the Bible, my life returned to normal for a while. Five months passed before I found myself sitting up in bed once again. I was unable to sleep.

At the age of fourteen I stood short at four feet ten, and I weighed about eighty-five pounds soaking wet. I was the smallest person entering the ninth grade, and I was terrified about my future in Seaholm High School. I was easily twenty pounds lighter and two inches shorter than everyone else in school; I was trying to figure out how I would survive the hallways of high school as the smallest ninth grader.

I was wide awake and worrying, so I pulled out the Bible a second time. Once again I was hoping to find peace. This time, however, I tried to be secretly strategic. In my head the Bible was just like every other great collection of stories; all the best stories would be in the back. So, as I "randomly" opened the dusty, unused Bible for the second time, I secretly hoped it would open up to one of the last pages. Sure enough, it opened up to Revelation 9:12. I will never forget the way I felt when I read the words that I expected would reassure me: "The first woe is past; two other woes are yet to come." Needless to say, I did not hear God. Instead, I heard my pastor's voice saying, "This is the Word of God for the people of God."

I thought, What kind of treasure is that? What does that even mean? Where is my assurance? peace? Where is the love of God?

I quickly closed the Bible back up. It had failed me. I did not open it again for about seven years.

Admittedly, the Bible is difficult to read. It is hard to understand. We read passages and cannot make any sense of them. The Bible is complex and confusing. To make matters worse, we always hear how central it is to our life and our ability to live fully, so we feel obligated to dive into the text regardless of our readiness. Sometimes this approach doesn't turn out very well.

We know we need Scripture, but wading into the deep waters of thousands of years can be intimidating. In order to live fully, however, we must be willing to wrestle with it, fight with it, work out our disagreements with it, and ultimately find peace with it.

Scripture as Spouse

John Wesley was known for saying, "All who desire the grace of God are to wait for it in searching the Scriptures." If we desire the love of God and if we desire God's abundance, we must spend time searching the Scriptures, which in many *love letter*

ways I consider to be God's love letter to humanity. While the Bible was penned by humans, it was inspired by the Holy Spirit and written in a way that we could read and constantly remember the many ways God has loved us throughout history.

God uses Scripture to speak to us. In this way, it becomes a living Word. Therefore, if we desire to love God, know God, and hear God's Word, we need to listen very intently to what God is saying. Just like any other relationship, the process of getting close to someone is difficult.

When I think about my deepest relationships, I think about my wife, Wendy. If you're married, chances are that your spouse inevitably says things that confuse you, challenge you, and make you wonder, What does that even mean? They will say things with which we disagree. But what would happen if we were to walk away from the people we love the most every time they said or did something we didn't understand or with which we didn't agree? The answer is simple: we wouldn't have any relationships at all. The same is true of our relationship with God.

The Bible is a mysterious book. The more we get to know it, the more we realize we don't know. It inspires and encourages, it frustrates and provokes, it is difficult and complex, but it is also wonderful, amazing, and life giving. No matter what happens or what we might read, living in pursuit of God requires that we stay in conversation with his Word. In order to grow in the knowledge and love of God, we must continue to wrestle with his love letter to creation.

I'm reminded of the story of Jacob (Isaac's son and Esau's brother) wrestling with God. In Genesis 32, Jacob was fleeing his older brother Esau's wrath. Family strife, a stolen blessing, and a number of other familial factors had led to Esau's vengeful pursuit of his twin brother. Esau was threatening death, and Jacob, the younger brother and heir apparent to Isaac's blessing, was scared. So with his wife, two maids, and eleven children, a frightened Jacob took off under the cover of night. When they reached the ford in Jabbok, Jacob sent his wife and children across the stream to continue on while he stayed behind to keep guard.

Scripture says,

That night Jacob got up and took his two wives, his two female servants and his eleven sons and crossed the ford of the Jabbok. After he had sent them across the stream, he sent over all his possessions. So Jacob was left alone, and a man wrestled with him till daybreak. When the man saw that he could not overpower him, he touched the socket of Jacob's hip so that his hip was wrenched as he wrestled with the man. Then the man said, "Let me go, for it is daybreak." But Jacob replied, "I will not let you go unless you bless me." The man asked him, "What is your name?" "Jacob," he answered. Then the man said, "Your name will no longer be Jacob, but Israel, because you have struggled with God and with humans and have overcome." Jacob said, "Please tell me your name." But he replied, "Why do you ask my name?" Then he blessed him there. So Jacob called the place Peniel, saying, "It is because I saw God face to face, and yet my life was spared." (Genesis 32:22-30)

Living fully requires that we stick it out. It requires that we wrestle with the tough questions like *Who am I?* and *Why am I here?* It requires that we wrestle with inconsistencies, with God's mystifying wisdom, until we are blessed. Wrestling means that we engage our hearts and minds in the reading of Scripture no matter how difficult it might be, because in and through our willingness to wrestle with the Word of God we will find blessing. If we do this, we will have life, peace, and purpose.

As we read Scripture and remember God's love letter, we will grow closer to God. In order to really engage Scripture, however, it is important to know what it is and how and why we read.

How We Read the Bible

John Wesley maintained that in order to love God, know God, and hear God, all we need is Scripture. The Bible is the primary source and criterion for all Christian teachings (doctrine). It is the seat upon which all things sit. Therefore, reading Scripture becomes a central means of grace. It is the primary avenue we travel down in order to encounter God. However, Wesley also says that we cannot simply examine Scripture in isolation. He often preached saying, "Scripture alone, but never alone." Therefore, Wesley believed that whenever we want to be positioned in the heart of God, all we have to do is begin to read (or sit on the seat).

It is worth noting that many Christians may discover that a scriptural seat sometimes needs legs. As we read the Bible, we often need to supplement our study with other God-centered disciplines, like prayer. I always pray before reading Scripture. I pray saying, "Fill me with your Holy Spirit that I might see and hear what you are saying to me today, God." I have found that praying this prayer heightens my understanding. It elevates my pursuit of the knowledge and love of God by invoking the Spirit.

Another way of heightening our understanding of God's Word—God's love letter—is by transforming our seat into a three-legged stool. We can do this by adding "legs" of deeper understanding. We'll call these legs *tradition, reason,* and *experience.* When we add tradition, reason, and experience into our reading of Scripture, we can elevate our faith and grow vertically in our relationship with God by improving our vantage point.

I like to think of reading Scripture like gardening. In order to grow healthy plants in a garden, you must utilize a variety of energy sources. You need fertilizer, sunlight, water, and so on. If you take away any one of those elements, the likelihood of having a healthy plant drops significantly. The same holds true for one's faith. As we read Scripture, we need to incorporate the best parts of tradition, experience, and reason; these, in addition to prayer, become our energy sources.

Tradition

When I read Scripture, one of the first things I do is compare what I am thinking with what others have thought. I solicit the advice of those who came before me. I employ their discovery and doctrine. I also look to the church fathers and the church's doctrine, or teaching. I compare what I read against doctrines of the Holy Trinity and the Apostles' Creed. These doctrines are rich treasures of tradition, so every time I look at Scripture, I do so alongside the tradition, thoughts, and teaching of thousands of years of scholarly commentary and insight.

Reason

Similarly, I seek to employ my reason in the same way. Our reason allows us the ability to confirm our understanding. While reason alone is useless without data from experience,

We need not check our brains at the door
to believe in God.

data alone is useless without the tool of reason. Reason allows us the ability to discuss and make sense of the Bible. Quite simply, the faculty of reason is a gift given to us to be used as an implement for deepening our faith. It provides the ability to be confirmed in our convictions. We need not check our brains at the door in order to believe in God; instead, believing in, knowing, and loving God requires that we think about and make sense of things using the gifts that we have been given—namely our reason. The caveat to this, of course, is that Scripture, and not reason, will always be the primary source.

Experience

Lastly, whenever I read Scripture, I always attempt to relate it to my own personal experiences. As he lived with us and walked among us, Jesus often used parables as teaching tools to reach people where they were. He spoke using stories, citing people, places, and things. Listeners could relate to his words. They had been in these situations. They understood his familiar language. Jesus spoke in this way to supplement their understanding of God's Word. It can do the same for us today. Our experiences should illumine our understanding of the living God. Whenever I read Scripture, I always ask myself, "How does this compare to my own experience of God? of life?"

That is how I approach Scripture. That is how I read it. I balance my own personal reading with tradition, biblical commentary, and church doctrine. I combine that with my experience of the Holy Spirit. I compare and reconcile whatever I read with my own personal experiences. And then I spend time thinking about it, talking about it, and growing in my understanding.

However, this approach to reading the Bible doesn't really address what happens in our holy book.

What Is the Bible?

I already noted that the Bible is the primary source and criterion for all Christian teaching. It is the seat upon which all things sit. Therefore, reading Scripture becomes a central means of grace (of receiving God's love). Scripture is the primary avenue we walk down in order to reach the very heart of God. It is the primary way God speaks to us.

The Bible, at its core, is more than a letter. It is a collection of writings and letters. My childhood pastor always said the Bible is more like a library than it is a book. The Bible is comprised of sixty-six different books written by a variety of authors in a variety of styles. Chronologically the Bible begins in the twelfth century BC and concludes in the second century AD. Some of the authors were poets, others were attorneys, others still were prophets, scribes, judges, tax collectors, tent builders, and orators. A few were even kings. Though they were diverse in background and lived in different geographic locales, all of these authors were bound together by the power of the Holy Spirit. They were all inspired by the Holy Spirit who flows through all things in such a way that reveals the glory of God.

When you open the Bible, one thing you may notice is that the Bible is divided in half. The first thirty-nine books make up the Old Testament, and the last twenty-seven books make up the New Testament. The Testaments are not ordered sequentially but rather are divided based on their proximity to the birth of Jesus Christ. "Testament" is simply another word for a promise shared between God and humanity. The Old

Testament focuses on the old covenants (promises) shared between God and humanity.

When we read the Old Testament, we discover God's promises of love and life as he worked through a variety of people, beginning with Adam and Eve. God created Adam and Eve, blessed them, and called them very good. Nevertheless, they turned away from God by doing the one thing they were not allowed to do. They ate from the tree of the knowledge of good and evil. They took a piece of fruit from God's tree. In so doing they rejected God. As a result, God kicked them out of the garden of Eden and began looking for others who might be willing to receive and live into the covenant. So God blessed Noah, and Noah did the same thing. Then there were Abraham and Sarah; they did the same thing. The same was true for Jacob, Isaac, Joseph, and Moses, a whole series of prophets, a collection of judges, and eventually the kings. The Old Testament follows God's pursuit of humanity all the way up until that promise is fulfilled and made new in Jesus Christ.

The New Testament begins with the birth of Christ, focuses on the new covenant, and describes the life thereafter. The first four books in the New Testament are called the Gospels. They are four different accounts of the life, death, and resurrection of Jesus Christ. The remaining twenty-three books in the New Testament are letters of history, instruction, and allegory that describe and point us toward what the Christian life should look like in a postresurrection world.

The story of Scripture, though divided into the Old and New, is intended to be one body of work from beginning to end. The two Testaments are meant to be read together because both are the story of God pursuing us through time. It is a story that never ends.

Why Do We Read the Bible?

We do not read Scripture to gain intellect. We do not read Scripture to have an advantage over another human being. We read Scripture so that we can move from literacy toward intimacy. We read Scripture in order to grow in our understanding of God's story—God's promise to all of creation throughout history—and find out how it relates to us. Our task in reading Scripture is simply to discover how we fit into this grand love story. To look at it another way, we read Scripture to see that we are a part of God's story. We—like Adam, Eve, and everyone who came after them—are the recipients of this amazing love and unfathomable grace. We read the Word of God and realize that grace is a gift and a task to live as those who are covered by the blood of the new covenant. We are free to live as one with God, each other, and in ministry to the whole world, loving and living sacrificially.

• • •

When I read the Old Testament, I read story after story of mistakes. I realize that my life, my tendencies, and my imperfect pursuits are nothing new to God. I identify with people like Jacob, a younger brother who sought the blessing reserved only for his older sibling. When I was a boy, I pursued blessing similarly. I wrestled for blessings. I was willing to do whatever it took to obtain what I believed I deserved.

I read Scripture, and Job's story resonates with me. Job was a person who spent time and endured what seemed like endless tragedies for an indiscernible end. When I read Job, I find hope and comfort because at times I have wondered what I did to deserve this. I have often wondered why things happen the way they do. Like everyone else, I sometimes wonder

We read scripture so we can move from literacy toward intimacy.

why bad things happen to good people and why some people's suffering seems unending. Whenever I witness or read about horrible tragedies, I sometimes find that I question God in the same way Job did.

I most certainly find comfort in reading about King David, the shepherd boy and runt of Jesse's litter. David was the least expected. He was the small guy nobody believed had the power to slay a giant. Admittedly, when I was a young man, I probably most closely identified with David. I felt like David on the soccer field. I felt like David in my family. I felt like David in the halls of Seaholm High School. I find strength reading his story.

Our task in reading the Old Testament is to follow God's promises of life and love as he worked with and through a variety of people, beginning with Adam and Eve in the garden of Eden. When we read their stories, it is easy to see that everything we experience has already happened to others, and God still loved them. So we read Scripture, relate it to our own circumstances, and take hope knowing that God will continue to love us, approach us, and pursue us, just as he has throughout history, even when we do the unthinkable and unexpected. Even then God will pursue us with his perfect love as he has throughout all of humanity from the beginning of time.

In Light of the Ending

The birth of Christ marks the beginning of the New Testament. In Christ's life, death, and resurrection we find a new covenant. Through Jesus Christ's body and blood, we find the fulfillment of all of God's past promises. The New Testament describes how God fulfills all of his old covenants through the life, death, and resurrection of Jesus Christ, his only Son and our Lord. Christians are to look at and read Scripture through the lens of Christ. We are to read Scripture in light of how it ends, namely with victory in Jesus. We are to search the Scriptures, remembering first how the story ends; with resurrection as our lens, we are to go back and reread the rest of the story to pick up on the subtle nuances and to gain a much deeper understanding of God's infinite depth of mercy and love. In light of the New Testament, all of the events of the Old Testament become dramatic rehearsals leading up to the deeds of Christ.

When we read Scripture all together (the Old and New Testaments), we begin seeing individual acts of love, moments of brilliance, key penalties, and unavoidable drama. We will see that God's movement throughout history has been amazing and that all of it comes together in order to point us to the fulfillment of God's promises of eternal life through the life, death, and resurrection of Jesus Christ. The Old Testament, and all of its drama, begins to make much more sense when we use the ending as our starting point and look at all things using Jesus Christ as our lens.

When we read the Bible, we ought to read it as one body of work from beginning to end in light of Jesus Christ. Jesus brings about unity as the Alpha and Omega, the beginning and the end. Living fully is about striving to see and encounter God in everyone and in everything. Reading Scripture helps us remember how and where God has moved throughout history. Upon reading this profound Word, we should begin to feel and know how deeply God loves us. This love culminated in the life, death, and resurrection of Jesus Christ, who came that we might live fully, love God with everything we have, and love our neighbors as ourselves.

Reading Scripture draws us nearer to this God. It plunges us into the story in a way that allows us to easily see and know God's presence and perfect love here and now. Jesus Christ, the Son of God, is found in the fullness of Scripture. Everything in it relates to his broken and beating heart. His love, his mercy, his grace are Scripture's sole object. Everything points to and reveals the perfect love of God and his mission of perfect communion. This is something the Pharisees (and many of us) don't understand whenever we approach Jesus or the Word of God.

In John 5, Jesus is approached by some law-abiding, Scripture-loving Pharisees. As Jesus and his disciples return to Galilee after being away, these Pharisees run up to the group in order to question Jesus about matters of the Law. The Pharisees argue with him about who he is and what he is doing. In their interrogation, they use Scripture against him in order to discredit him and to reveal their own in-depth knowledge of Scripture. However, their tactic turns out to be a careless, foolish, and overly optimistic one.

Jesus replies to them saying, "You study the Scriptures diligently because you think that in them you have eternal life. These are the very Scriptures that testify about me, yet you refuse to come to me to have life" (John 5:39-40).

When we read Scripture we equip ourselves to see God standing right before us wherever we go and in whatever situation we find ourselves. Scripture allows us to live fully by reminding us that God loves us wholly and has since the very beginning.

You study the Scriptures diligently because you think that in them you have eternal life. These are the Scriptures that testify about me, yet you refuse to come to me to have life.

John 5:39-40

1. The Old and New Testaments can be translated as the Old and New Promises. What promises has God given you through Scripture? For what promises are you still waiting?

2. The author refers to the Bible as God's love letter to humanity. Do you read it this way? How would reading Scripture through a lens of God's extravagant love change the way you interpret the Word?

3. We see clearly in Scripture that God is always using broken and messed up people to reveal his love for mankind. Who are Biblical characters that have been compelling examples of God's grace?

Making Friends Out of Strangers

"For where two or three gather in my name, there am I with them."

—Matthew 18:20

Missional living begins with worship. When we worship, we meet God, fall to our knees, and acknowledge that God is God and we are not. Worship helps us see the world as a gift given to us through which we might take every moment as an opportunity to join in God's mission of perfect communion, love God with everything we have and all that we are, and live lives that sing of God's glory.

Worship opens our eyes to the new reality that the world is the Lord's and everything in it, and Scripture reinforces this belief. We read Scripture to remember and give thanks for the ways in which God loves us unconditionally and has from the beginning of time. The missional life starts taking shape, however, when we reach out in love toward our neighbors, loving them as ourselves, and turning strangers into friends. Living fully looks like building Christian community through love-filled relationships in the hope that others might encounter God, be filled, and then go and do likewise.

This might sound easy to do, but sometimes the easiest practices are the hardest to live out.

Leprosy and Loneliness

Naaman the Great was a leader in the Syrian army in the days of Elisha. By his powerful sword he delivered a great victory over Israel. On top of it all he was unimaginably wealthy. Naaman seemingly had it all. Yet, as it usually happens in life, this wasn't the whole story. Naaman the Great was actually Naaman the Flawed. Naaman was a leper and was slowly dying. He was alone because of it. Not only was leprosy a debilitating disease, but culturally lepers were also treated as outcasts, both hopeless and helpless.

ENTOURAGE

The same was true of Naaman: he commanded men who were trained to do whatever he demanded of them, but he had no friends. Considering all of his power Naaman still lacked a community of support. Naaman structured his life this way intentionally because if anybody found out that he was a leper, he would have lost everything. His achievements would have been discredited and long forgotten. When Naaman wasn't busy fighting, he was busy trying to conceal his illness. In 2 Kings 5, Naaman was desperate to find a solution that would help him live fully.

Naaman wondered just like the rest of us, *What must I do to live fully?* Sitting all by himself on his throne one day, secretly wrestling over how much longer he could continue to mask his illness, Naaman saw a servant girl whispering quietly to his wife. She whispered, "My lord, if only he visited the prophet in Samaria. He would be cured."

Naaman couldn't hear what she was saying, but his insecurities got the best of him. Naaman barked at his wife, "What did she say to you, woman?"

Naaman's wife barked right back at him, "She said you're sick, Naaman, and everyone knows it! She also said that she knows someone who's willing to help you." Without another word, Naaman hopped off his throne, quickly gathered together his entourage of chariots, horses, and soldiers, grabbed a supply of gold and silver, and was ready to do whatever it took to find a cure so that he could stop hiding and start living again. Little did he know he wouldn't need his entourage or his wealth.

The entourage made a few stops along the way before arriving at the prophet Elisha's house. Once there, he rang the doorbell, but there was no answer. Instead, from behind closed doors, Elisha called out a message, saying, "Naaman, I know why you're here; go jump in that river. You know, the Jordan? Do that seven times and you'll be cured."

Rather than saying, "Thank you," and jumping into the river, Naaman became enraged with Elisha. "How's that going to help anything? This is ridiculous! I might have been willing to listen to a servant girl. I might have been willing to travel all the way from Damascus to find you, Elisha, but now I'm supposed to jump into a puddle of mud seven times because you told me to? Not a chance. That's crazy talk!" Naaman ranted, "If I had known all I needed to do was jump in a river, then I would have done it on my own. I would have jumped into one of my own rivers in Syria."

Elisha refused to respond. He didn't utter another word. Silence descended upon Naaman's entourage. And Naaman didn't know what to do. The great general continued to stand outside Elisha's home in stubborn defiance. Thankfully, another one of his servants had the courage to speak up. He said to Naaman, "If the prophet had commanded you to do something difficult, would you not have done it? How much more, when all he said to you was, 'Wash and be clean'?" (v. 13).

That was difficult for Naaman to hear, but the servant was right. Naaman jumped into the river seven times as instructed. Though he had no friends, Naaman found himself surrounded and guided by loyal and devoted servants who, by their presence, brought forth healing. They saved his life.

Sometimes I wonder what choice Naaman might have made had he not been surrounded by loving and devoted servants. Where would Naaman have been without a community of humble followers? They helped him find the life he was looking for. This is what it looks like to love others. When we learn how to love our neighbors as ourselves, we discover abundant life.

In Matthew 22, the Pharisees approach Jesus and ask him for the secret to life. "What can we do?" they ask. "How can we live to experience abundant life?"

The Pharisees were scholars who traditionally adhered to all the complex biblical rules. They were people like Naaman, focused on careers, accomplishments, and being great in the eyes of society and correct in their interpretation of the Law. In Matthew 22, when the Pharisees ask Jesus to explain the meaning of life, they ask, "Teacher, which is the greatest commandment?" (v. 36).

Christ replies by telling them that the secret to life is simple: "'Love the Lord your God with all your heart and with all your soul and with all your mind.' This is the first and greatest commandment. And the second is like it: 'Love your neighbor as yourself'" (vv. 37-39).

Jesus Christ came into the world that we might become one with God, one with each other, and one in ministry to all the world. God's mission through Jesus Christ is perfect communion, which requires the perfect love of God and the perfect love of neighbor. Jesus came that we might have life and have it abundantly; this is possible when we form and build beloved community no matter where we are. Naaman's community gave him life. Yours will as well if you are willing to love your neighbors as yourself and make friends out of strangers.

Living fully demands that we open up to others and give all that we are and all that we have in the same way that Jesus Christ did for the world. Our ongoing loving relationships possess the power to change the world. To be missional is to be in relationship. We are created to be in relationship with others. From the beginning of time, after God spoke everything into being, the very next thing he did is let us know that he created us for relationships.

It is not good when we are alone. We need helpers, partners, and companions. We need community.

The Happiness Project

People generally feel happier when they are with other people. Gretchen Rubin, author of *The Happiness Project*, writes, "Studies show that if you have five or more friends with whom you discuss an important matter, you're far more likely to describe yourself as 'very happy.' At the same time, no matter what they're doing, people tend to feel happier when they're with other people . . . whether you're exercising, commuting or doing housework, everything is more fun in company. And this is true not just of extroverts but, perhaps surprisingly, of introverts as well."

Research indicates that out of fifteen daily activities, there is only one activity during which people are happier alone rather than with other people—that activity is praying. I would even argue with that one. Prayer is a conversation with another being, God. We are happier when we're in relationship with others because this is how we were designed to function.

Jesus assures us that regardless of where we are in life, whether we are in the midst of confusion, struggle, or strife, all we must do is gather together among others, and he'll be there. This is phenomenal news because no matter what we are facing, God promises to be with us: we will be able to survive our

*we will be able to survive
our trials as long as we
are in community*

trials as long as we are in community. Living fully, therefore, requires that we form authentic, love-filled relationships.

Augustine describes our desire to be in relationship as what makes us human. We are social animals who are drawn toward each other, and so we live in a world filled with and ordered by relational and social networks. If ever there were a time that revealed this dimension of the missional life, it would have to be now. It seems that we cannot go anywhere anymore to escape relationships thanks to the various social networks on the Internet.

Updated from My Mobile

Since 1997, social networking sites have become significant and promising tools that help us live fully. If used correctly, social networking sites enable us to connect with all sorts of people across great distances. When disasters strike, we can find out immediate information about loved ones and take comfort knowing they are safe. We can organize massive fund-raising and relief efforts to meet the needs of those who are hurting or struggling. We can retain and rekindle past relationships and connections that we would have otherwise lost due to long-distance moves, life transitions, or circumstance. High school friends are reuniting, large families are staying up to date, and people are finding love with relative ease (two-thirds of the weddings I have performed in the past five years have come from social networking site connections).

Moreover, for those who struggle with crowds or for those with disabilities, social media helps them overcome social anxieties and physical barriers in order to connect. Most importantly though, social networking sites remind us that our relationships matter.

However, in our attempts to be increasingly relational we have created unintentional barriers. We have made it harder to live fully. Last week I was driving past a movie theater and I noticed a group of twentysomethings standing out front. They happened to be standing in a circle, and all of them were staring at their phones. I stopped. I got out of my car, walked up to them, and asked them what they were doing.

After they got past the shock that someone had actually addressed them using spoken words, they told me that they were updating their statuses on their Facebook pages. I smiled and thanked them for sharing. As I walked back to my car, I chuckled, wondering whether that is what God envisioned when he said, "Where two or three are gathered in my name, I am there" (Matthew 18:20, NRSV). Is that community? Is that friendship? Is that how deep meaningful relationships work?

I went out to eat a week later. As I ate, I noticed a couple sitting at the table next to me. As they sat across from each other, waiting for supper, both of their heads were bowed. At first I thought they were praying, but soon I realized that they were simply checking their smartphones. Is that what friends do? Is that what a married couple does? Is that community? Were they connecting? Is that what God intends for us?

Another time I was at a Detroit Tigers game; as I watched the game, I was distracted by a group of men a couple rows in front of me who seemed to be disinterested in the action. I studied them more closely only to realize that they were on their phones tracking their Fantasy Baseball accounts. They were sitting at a game together, in the midst of a crowd, but were totally removed from its power.

I bet you've experienced moments like these as well. Is this even how you behave around others?

I received

557 birthday greetings

posted to my Facebook wall,

but no one made me a cake.

In our attempts to build relationships, it has become easier for us to hide behind our social networks than to engage in love-filled friendships. It has become easier to get lost in our social networks than it is to live the missional life and step out into the lives of those around us. We've found that it's easier to live like Naaman or the Pharisees, alone and isolated, than to act like one of the servants or to pick up our cross and follow Christ.

How do you spend your time in public? Do you hide behind your smartphone instead of talking with others?

I have seen several folks walk into our downtown church, and rather than talk with the people around them or greet them with a handshake or embrace, they walk into worship with their eyes fixed on their screens and their thumbs flying over their keyboards. It is becoming easier and easier to hide behind our social networks. When we do, we experience a thin version of community, often from the comforts of our own home. It is increasingly difficult to get out there and live fully in the world that God has gifted to us.

Social networks and technology are beneficial because they allow us an amazing quantity of "friends." But the quality of our off-line friendships is diminishing. My guess is that there are people who might have a thousand Facebook friends but still feel profoundly lonely.

We can have thousands of online friends, but in our moments of greatest need or celebration, we have none. This past year I received 557 birthday greetings posted to my Facebook wall, but no one made me a cake or gave me a gift. And there were definitely no hugs. It made me feel strange and empty. It felt like the opposite of Jesus' purpose and mission of abundant life.

In a study recently published, sociologists found that between 1985 and 2004 the average American's number of close confidants declined from three to two and that those reporting "no close confidants" jumped from 10 percent to 25 percent. We are all in need of ongoing loving relationships. It's as simple as that. We were created, we are here, and we are living on earth that we might be engaged in a collection of ongoing loving relationships. In order to do this we need to work at it.

The missional life requires that we constantly attempt to make friends out of strangers. Missional living requires that we love our neighbors as much as we love ourselves. In order to find and make friends we must be willing to open up, risk rejection, and give ourselves away. There is more in giving than receiving. Missional living begins in worship, but it subsists based on our ability to love others sacrificially.

In his letter to the Philippians, Paul describes for us what this looks like. In fact, he says it looks a lot like Jesus,

who, being in very nature God, did not consider equality with God something to be used to his own advantage; rather, he made himself nothing by taking the very nature of a servant, being made in human likeness. And being found in appearance as a man, he humbled himself by becoming obedient to death—even death on a cross! (2:6-8)

In the gospel of John, Jesus states that, "Greater love has no one than this: to lay down one's life for one's friends" (15:13). The missional life is rooted in the pursuit and formation of ongoing loving relationships. These friendships are rooted in sacrificial love. When we share and receive Christ-like, sacrificial love, we, through our Lord and Savior, have the power to change the world.

Community as Hole-in-Roof

Brian and Kate were a young couple who had been coming to Resurrection Downtown for some time. Neither of them had ever really been a part of an active, worshiping congregation, an authentic loving community where they felt connected or supported. Both were extremely successful individuals. Kate was a director at a large Fortune 100 company, and Brian owned his own business. They had done much that society deems right, yet they felt alone.

I remember talking to Brian and Kate over dinner one night; both of them expressed a deep desire to get plugged into a network of friends. They wanted to find a group of friends with whom they could share life. They wanted to be in a community where they could grow, learn, suffer, and celebrate. They were looking for connection, meaning, and purpose.

At the end of the dinner I invited them to consider joining a small group, a community of friends who meet weekly to grow closer with each other and with God through study and service. Neither of them was excited about this idea at first. It was too structured. It required commitment. Kate told me it was "too cheesy." She might have even rolled her eyes. Ultimately, however, they agreed to give it a shot. After all, they were searching for meaning and purpose, and this was a simple solution. What more could they ask for?

Brian and Kate had been meeting with their small group for about eight weeks when tragedy struck. Kate fell at church, hit her head, broke bones, lost memory, and was suddenly facing a future filled with multiple surgeries. In the days that followed this accident, Brian and Kate were paralyzed with fear. They needed strength and assurance. They needed healing, and they needed God. Without hesitation their small-group community surrounded and enveloped them. In fact, the supportive presence of her small-group community was so powerful that, to this day, Kate doesn't remember how she fell; she only remembers how she felt when she opened her eyes in the hospital to a community of friends surrounding her in prayer.

Kate and Brian have discovered that living fully involves other people. Living fully involves radical hospitality, loving our neighbors, and making friends out of strangers. Kate's community of neighbors and friends, all of whom had been strangers just weeks earlier, supported them unconditionally in moments of great need. They picked her up when she was not able to pick herself up. They cared for Brian when he couldn't care for himself. Together the small group of former strangers brought forth new purpose and a future filled with hope. Brian and Kate now live for others in that same kind of way. Here's an excerpt of what she wrote to that group a year into her recovery.

> *At around 11 p.m. this day last year, I came to in a hospital with all of you surrounding me. I had no idea how I'd gotten there and why my head and mouth hurt so much.*
>
> *As the days passed, I was humbled to learn of your acts of kindness. You went to my house to pack me a bag (of clothes). You brought me flowers and food. You cared for my husband. You patiently answered my questions (over and over and over). You made sure I was never alone at the hospital. You prayed for my recovery. You sent me encouraging emails and texts. You helped me conquer my fear of the dentist.*

I have no memory of ten hours that day. But I will never forget your acts of kindness.

Thank you for being there.

Kate

Kate has a new purpose. Together, she and Brian now have a mission to "go and do likewise." They have direction. They now live as some of our community's most faithful small-group leaders. They continue to welcome others into similar love-filled communities that are collectively joining in God's mission for all of creation. That mission is perfect communion. They now lead missional lives and seek to make friends of strangers by offering up their lives, sacrificially, in love toward others. My guess is that a similar event happened to a man described in the second chapter of Mark.

In Mark 2, by the time Jesus arrives in Capernaum, the crowds are ready and waiting for him. The anticipation is palpable. An energy is running through the whole town. Nearly everyone has turned out. The lone exception is a paralytic lying in the street. We don't really know what has caused his paralysis. He could be paralyzed with fear, anxiety, or doubt. Maybe he is struggling with loneliness. We don't know much about the man except that he is not well.

But then four friends come to the house where Jesus is, bringing the paralyzed man with them. Four friends have apparently come to the rescue. In a very dark hour, when he needs it most, they literally pick him up. They physically carry him into the house where Jesus is. But they can't fit through the front door because of the crowds, so they decide to try the next best thing. These friends climb up to the roof, dragging their friend with them, and then, making a hole in the roof over Jesus' head, they let down the mat on which the man lies.

The friends are taking a huge risk in approaching the Son of God this way. They are giving all they have to their neighbor. Because of their risk, this nameless paralytic is able to see Jesus. When Jesus sees him, the paralytic is healed because of *their* faith and *their* love. Jesus says to the paralytic, "Son, your sins are forgiven" (v. 5). And the newly forgiven man stands up and immediately takes the mat and goes out before all of them. Everyone there is amazed, and they start worshiping God, saying, "We have never seen anything like this!" (v. 12). This is the power of community. This is abundant life.

Koinōnia

Living fully unlocks the power of God in the community. The missional life has everything to do with improving the quality of our relationships. It is about opening up a depth of mercy for others and not always expanding the breadth of our connections. A missional life strives to love God with everything we have and love our neighbors as ourselves; it is rooted in the example of Christ and our corresponding willingness to abandon all that we have and all that we are in order to befriend others, love them, and connect with those around us. Missional living is rooted in sacrifice, the perfect love of God, and the grace of Jesus Christ.

The Greek word for community is *koinōnia*. It is used roughly twenty times in Scripture and found only in the New Testament. Every time it is mentioned, it refers to the character of the early church. Most often it is translated as "fellowship" or "communion." It is most commonly used to imply or describe the Christian community. We hear about this

EVERYTHING IN COMMON

koinōnia kind of community in Acts 2:42-47. Read how one ancient Christian community is described:

> They devoted themselves to the apostles' teaching and to fellowship, to the breaking of bread and to prayer. Everyone was filled with awe at the many wonders and signs performed by the apostles. All the believers were together and had everything in common. They sold property and possessions to give to anyone who had need. Every day they continued to meet together in the temple courts. They broke bread in their homes and ate together with glad and sincere hearts, praising God and enjoying the favor of all the people. And the Lord added to their number daily those who were being saved.

The earliest Christians were devoted to their communities, to each other, to Scripture, to the breaking of bread, and to prayer. The earliest churches were focused purely on the depth and quality (not breadth and quantity) of their relationships. They were focused on doing life together no matter what. They were committed to a common purpose. They shared a vision, and they traveled together through life's ups and downs, wherever their journey took them. They loved each other unconditionally. They didn't pay any attention to the number of friends they had; instead, they focused on doing whatever it took in order that those around them would feel loved, would connect with Christ, and would be blessed by abundant life. These communities embodied the grace of God as they loved one another with reckless abandon.

Leading a missional life requires building Christian community wherever we go so that all people can experience the love of God and in turn become deeply committed themselves. This happens when we wholly give ourselves to the business of loving God with everything we have and loving our neighbors as ourselves. Living a missional life is realizing that God is God and we are not and then seeing our mission as though it were a part of God's mission for all of creation. It is striving after this picture of perfect communion, where all become one with God, one with each other, and one in ministry to all the world.

Whenever I think about my loving relationships, I always get caught up remembering the many men and women in my life who have passed away. I thank God for them, and I spend quite a bit of time remembering them. In fact, when I write, I think about my grandmother Dorothy. When I think of her, I do not remember any of Dorothy's Facebook posts or text messages (though she texted and posted all the time). What I remember are the quality times I spent with her. I especially remember speaking with her, hugging her, and drinking coffee with her. She always showed up for me. She was always present and available.

The gospel of Matthew teaches that to be Christian is to be bound together in community. Being bound together requires that we show up for each other. We must participate in the lives of those around us. We must do so even when it is inconvenient, when there are disagreements, and especially when it is not easy.

When I think about things I regret in life, they never involve instances or memories of the times when I actually participated in someone else's life. I never regret the times I showed up in support of folks at the hospital. I have never regretted showing up for worship, even though there have been times when it would have been easier to stay at home. I never regret attending concerts, baseball games, service projects, or small groups. You know what I do regret? I regret the times when I remained aloof. I regret the times when I sent an email or a text instead of showing up or calling or driving to meet someone.

The missional life is about showing up and engaging in deep, meaningful relationships. It is about opening our eyes that we might see God dancing in the midst of our communities, among the strangers, neighbors, and friends surrounding us.

So here is a question for you: When was the last time you showed up for someone and regretted it? Jesus showed up that we might have life and have it abundantly. When was the last time you showed up for someone to offer him or her life? If you cannot think of one, I wholeheartedly encourage you to look for and take advantage of the next opportunity.

When is the last time you ventured out into the community and made an attempt to integrate yourself? Are you a part of a community group? Are you connected to a church? Have you blessed any of your neighbors? Do you have any friends or relatives that are in need of community? If you are looking for meaning or purpose, if you are searching for abundant life, maybe you should call them or send them a nice handwritten note. Or perhaps what God is really calling you to do is to simply show up in their life. Meet them where they are, as they are, in the way that Christ meets us as Emmanuel. If you do, I promise you won't regret it.

At the most critical juncture in his life, Jesus did not sit in his bedroom posting status updates for all the world to see. He did not email his final words. Instead, he sought the comfort of his authentic, love-filled community in the Upper Room. Jesus gathered his friends together that they might laugh, love, share a meal, and help the rest of the world realize that it's only in the context of community—in the act of breaking bread together as friends—that we can see God's perfect presence in our midst, which leads us to the next dimension of the missional life—breaking bread.

1. God has commanded his blessing where people live in unity with one another (Psalm 133). Why do you think his blessing is reserved for community? In what ways do you see God's blessing through fellowship?

2. The author writes about friendship as "opening up a depth of mercy for others." Do you view your friendships this way? Reflect on the people in your life. How might God be calling you to be merciful to them?

3. In what ways would our relationships change if they were covenantal (promise based) rather than contractual (circumstantial/performance based)?

Breaking Bread

"Then Jesus declared, 'I am the bread of life. Whoever comes to me will never go hungry, and whoever believes in me will never be thirsty.'"

—John 6:35

On Easter Sunday Christ rose from the dead, conquered the grave, reconciled the nations, surpassed everyone's expectations, and gave us reason to celebrate. Easter is a time for rejoicing, for singing alleluias to our King. On Easter Sunday we find hope. We realize that the worst thing going on in our lives is never the last thing. We realize that death doesn't win. The risen Christ declares that God's amazing love, not death, wins.

For me, that is exactly what Easter Sunday felt like as a child. My mother always decorated the house with bright pinks and greens. We couldn't go anywhere in our home without feeling happy and hopeful. All was bright and beautiful, and the whole house was filled with the love and light of Christ (and the Easter Bunny, of course).

A professor of mine at Duke Divinity School once said that our goal as Christians should be to celebrate the resurrection every Sunday. Every Sunday, he believed, should feel like Easter. He actually went on to say that Christians shouldn't stop there, but that we should strive to celebrate Easter every day, not just every Sunday.

Have you ever wondered what it would take for people to celebrate Easter every Sunday or even every day?

What would it take for you to walk around announcing, singing, and believing that "Christ is risen!" the way we do on Easter Sunday? What would it take for you to be like Christ's disciples, who, on the road to Emmaus, ran into Jerusalem shouting, "We have seen him! He's alive: we've met the living God!"

This is the goal of the missional life. This is seeing Superman in our midst. This is living in pursuit of God.

Every day should be a day in which we hope and expect to encounter the living God. Every day should feel as though we've met the risen Christ. Carrying or forming these expectations is a part of being fully alive, fully present, and filled with the love of God. Living fully is living in the knowledge that there isn't anything we can or can't do that could ever separate us from the love of God. When we live missionally, we realize that God loves us and there's nothing we can do about it.

For the past few years I have surveyed most of the congregation in order to uncover what makes Easter such a special day for them. I have received a variety of answers. Some have commented on how everything seems brighter on Easter. Some have talked about the feeling of new life and new beginnings. Some have mentioned how they like that everyone seems to smile on Easter. Some have talked about the flowers. As I processed the answers, a pattern began to emerge.

Even though I asked people to name the "one thing" that makes Easter special, everyone was giving me multiple answers. Furthermore, there were some unexpected consistencies. Out of the four hundred people I polled, over 98 percent of them told me about the meals they shared with family and friends on Easter. They told me about the food they ate.

I heard story after story about the delicious, extravagant, home-cooked meals served on kitchen tables, which often needed all the extra leaves to accommodate food. I heard about prime rib steaks and horseradish, roasted lamb with mint sauce, HoneyBaked Ham with mashed potatoes, green beans, beef brisket, barbecue, deviled eggs, fruit salad, and potato salad.

It quickly became clear to me: in a majority of homes, Easter is partially celebrated with special food. Therefore, replicating Easter and living fully has to involve large amounts of good food and some really heavy-duty kitchen tables.

As a pastor, a part of me expects and hopes that people encounter God every Sunday in worship or, if not worship, in Scripture, prayer, or community. In reality, when it comes right down to it, one of the best places to meet God is at the dinner table. Though pastors pine after the sacred and holy, God usually meets us where we are, as we are. Dinner tables are just one of those places. No matter who we are or where we are, we tend to be present at the dinner table. At the dinner table, we are hungry for more and ready to eat.

On Easter evening, the disciples were dejected and depressed. They walked home from Calvary with their heads in their hands and their hearts twisted in grief. In the midst of their journey, a stranger (who was actually the risen Christ) joined them on the road and started talking with them. They were having a holy conversation, but they did not really know what was going on. They were crippled with grief, walking in darkness, and unsure of what their future held.

The disciples were walking and conversing with a stranger, but they were unaware of his importance. They were doing the very same thing they had been doing week in and week out for the past three years. The disciples had walked and talked with Jesus all across Israel, but on Easter evening, they couldn't see who it was who journeyed with them.

On Easter Sunday, the disciples couldn't see Jesus. They were engaged in a routine, possibly boring, conversation with a stranger. That Sunday had yet to become Easter Sunday. They had yet to experience the hope of the resurrection. They hadn't truly encountered God, even though he was walking right beside them. The disciples did not begin living until they invited this stranger over to share a meal. That's when they began to *live*.

The worst thing going on in our lives is never the last thing.

As they gathered around the kitchen table, surrounded by their friends and family, this stranger was given the seat of honor as the invited guest. Sitting around the table, this stranger picked up the customary loaf of bread. He blessed it, broke it, and then began handing it out in the same way he had just three nights earlier. As he did, the disciples' eyes were opened as though they were seeing things for the very first time. Because of the bread, the disciples finally saw who had been with them the entire time. They saw the risen Christ. They saw their rabbi. They finally came face-to-face with the living God, and in that moment (and not a second before), Sunday became Easter Sunday.

Luke recounts it this way: "When he was at the table with them, he took bread, gave thanks, broke it and began to give it to them" (Luke 24:30). Before they sat down at the table for dinner, the disciples were depressed, dejected, and walking home in despair. They were frustrated by the fact that they'd have to go back to their old jobs and return to the status quo. The moment they sat down at the table to break bread with strangers and friends, however, they saw God again and were filled with hope.

This was such a dramatic encounter that the disciples immediately jumped up from the table to run as fast as they could back to Jerusalem, which was a seven-mile journey, in the middle of the night, in order to share the news with their friends. They proclaimed breathlessly, "We've seen him; he is risen! He is risen indeed!"

Luke writes that the disciples told the others "how Jesus was recognized by them when he broke the bread" (v. 35). I wonder what the disciples would have said if I went back and asked them what made Easter Sunday so special to them? My guess is that they would mention the meal.

The breaking of the bread is powerful. Breaking bread is essential to life, but it's also an essential dimension to the missional life. For centuries, Christians have recognized the presence of Jesus Christ or have seen God in communal meals. We meet God every time we gather together to eat and drink.

The Communion Life

For the church, partaking in the communal meal is a sacred event. We call it Holy Communion. Holy Communion is a sacrament, an outward and visible sign of an inward and spiritual grace. It is a sign of the covenant that God shares with his people, the primary channel through which people meet and experience the promises of God in Jesus Christ. In most churches, Communion is a sacrament.

Sacrament comes from the Latin word *sacramentum*. It's a term that is most commonly understood to mean "promise." Sacraments are the promises of God. Through the breaking of bread at a communal table, we remember that God promises us a life that never ends. We don't know how this happens. We cannot comprehend why, but at the table on Easter Sunday, Jesus appears before us to offer us his light, hope, and promise of abundant life through the breaking of bread. This is nothing short of a holy mystery, which closely resembles the Greek word for sacrament, *mysterion*. God's promises are often mysterious. This meal is a mystery.

There are a variety of explanations that attempt to unpack exactly how Communion brings us life. When it comes to God's promises and the inner workings of his grace, we can't help but throw up our hands, acknowledging that this is a divine mystery under the auspices of the Holy Spirit and that we will never untangle or comprehend it.

Some people refer to Communion as the Eucharist, which means "thanksgiving." The Eucharist is a meal during which we give thanks for all the ways Christ sacrificed for us. We give thanks for the gift of forgiveness and the promise of salvation. In our community in downtown Kansas City, we celebrate this meal on a weekly basis, following a liturgy of thankfulness. Every week we take time to give thanks for the many ways in which God has worked throughout history to reconcile us with each other and with him. Celebrating the Eucharist is a way of celebrating Easter. It is a way of reminding us that God loves us and never lets us go, no matter who we are, where we have come from, or what we have done to get there. Even when we're twisted in grief and stumbling about in the darkness, God always finds us and invites us to join him for supper.

Some people refer to this meal as the Lord's Supper, which is a means of remembering the Last Supper, where Jesus, on the night in which he gave himself up for us, gathered with his friends to share his last meal. When we break bread together, we remember that fateful night when Jesus chose to eat a traditional Passover meal with his friends rather than run away. He knows the next day he will take his place as the Lamb of God. He foreshadows this inevitability as he tells his disciples, "Take. Eat. This is my body given for you. This is my blood poured out for you."

Others simply call this meal Communion, which paints images of the gathered community coming together in order to become one with each other and one with God. Communion shapes and forms community. In Communion the heart of God is poured out for all of creation. Those communities are then formed by collections and networks of companions where people love and care for each other with a similar kind of love. Breaking bread transforms strangers into companions, and in this way Communion gives shape to and paves the way for God's vision of beloved community.

Whether you call it the Eucharist, Holy Communion, the Lord's Supper, or simply the breaking of bread, this meal was for the earliest Christians and remains for us the greatest channel by which we connect with God. Communion is a simple meal with simple food at a simple table, but it has the power to shape who we are as companions, and it enables us to meet God in profound ways. Breaking bread is an important dimension of the missional life because it allows us to be filled in a very real way with God's abundant life.

However, it is worth noting that when I ask people about their experiences of this simple meal with simple food at a simple table, I rarely hear about stories of profound transformation or holy encounters or depth. Instead I hear a collection of bloopers: I think this is because Communion is pretty confusing for most.

My mother remembered her very first experience of Communion and shared it with me. It was such a powerful experience that she still thinks of it every time she breaks bread. She was sitting at a Maundy Thursday service with her sister (my aunt), in which the Last Supper is generally reenacted. Her church was one that served Communion, not with bread and wine, but with thin wafers and grape juice.

The usher pointed to her pew, so she and her sister walked reverently to the Communion station filled with anticipation and excitement. This was the first time they had

HOLY PROJECTILE

received Communion in the big church. Both made it up to the front and held out their hands. The pastor handed them the wafer. They held it reverently and moved to dip the wafer (the body of Christ) into the cup of grape juice (Christ's blood). They quickly popped the juice and the wafer into their mouths and walked back to their seats.

As the pair sat down, they both should have breathed an easy sigh of relief. To all appearances, both my mom and my aunt had made it through their first Communion. However, rather than basking in the glow of their first Communion, my mother secretly waged an inner battle. The wafer had gotten stuck to the roof of her mouth, and she couldn't get it out. She tried to pry it loose with her tongue, nervously looking around to see if anyone was watching her. Nobody had noticed her discomfort yet, so she did what we all would have done in that situation. She stuck her finger up into her mouth in the hopes of prying the juice-soaked wafer free.

As she worked the wafer free, she unintentionally flung it out of her mouth and onto the back of the woman sitting in the pew in front of her. And there it rested, the body of Christ on the back of the woman sitting in front of her, who luckily hadn't felt the impact of the holy projectile.

My mother was mortified. For the next thirty years she avoided receiving Communion.

Not everyone has had an experience of Communion like my mother's, but my guess is that you've struggled to understand the importance of breaking bread in the pursuit of abundant life. Communion is confusing. People have a diffi-cult time comprehending how food made by humans somehow becomes the body of our God. We struggle to understand why we must eat something that represents God in order to commune with him. The truth of the matter is this—Communion is not really about the food. It is about meeting God.

Old and New Bread

God uses bread to connect with his people in both the Old and New Testaments. In the Old Testament, in Exodus 16, the Israelites are wandering through the desert. Moses has freed them from the bonds of Egyptian slavery. God leads his people to their freedom through the Red Sea, first by parting the water and then by leading them with a pillar of cloud by day and fire by night. But just a few weeks after the Israelites had miraculously escaped Egyptian persecution, they lose their faith in God. Grumbling about their disconnectedness, they shout at Moses, saying,

> "If only we had died by the LORD's hand in Egypt! There we sat around pots of meat and ate all the food we wanted, but you have brought us out into this desert to starve this entire assembly to death." Then the LORD said to Moses, "I will rain down bread from heaven for you. The people are to go out each day and gather enough for that day. In this way I will test them and see whether they will follow my instructions. On the sixth day they are to prepare what they bring in, and that is to be twice as much as they gather on the other days." So Moses and Aaron said to all the Israelites, "In the evening you will know that it was the LORD who brought you out of Egypt, and in the morning you will see the glory of the LORD, because he has heard your grumbling against him. Who are we, that you should grumble against us?" (vv. 3-7)

God uses bread, in this case manna from heaven, to open the Israelites' eyes that they might see the glory of the

Lord. This isn't a story about bread; it is a story about God using bread to meet his people.

The same kind of thing happens to Elijah in the wilderness. He wanders through the wilderness for three years before he finally resigns himself to die. At his lowest point, under the cover of a shrub, an angel of God appears to him offering him bread in the hope that he will pick it up, carry on, and encounter the presence of God.

God reveals himself to Elijah through the sharing of a meal. Similar to the Israelites, Elijah's bread is bread for the journey; it is bread for the road ahead, the vehicle that enables Elijah to carry on to the place where God eventually speaks to him.

Throughout the Gospels, Jesus repeatedly uses miracles involving bread as a means of demonstrating the power of God and revealing his identity so that people might come to trust and believe in him. Aside from the resurrection, there is only one miracle that appears in all four Gospels: the feeding of the five thousand. However, although this miracle involves bread, what's most interesting is what happens afterward. In the aftermath of this miracle, Jesus withdraws knowing that crowds will follow him. He knows they will want more from him soon, and he is right.

The very next day the crowds begin searching for him. By the time they find him, they are hungry for more. In John 6, Jesus tells the crowd, "Very truly I tell you, you are looking for me, not because you saw the signs I performed but because you ate the loaves and had your fill" (v. 26). In essence Jesus is telling them, "I fed you once that you might see me for who I am, but now you come to me, not to worship, not to join me, but rather to eat more. All you want is food, but I have plans much greater than food to offer you."

Jesus is trying to teach them that the miracles he is performing and the life he is living are about something much greater than filling their stomachs. Rather, he desires to teach them about their lives, about who they are and why they are on earth. Though the miracle involves bread, Jesus wants to reveal God's glory to all the world.

So they asked him, "What sign then will you give that we may see it and believe you? What will you do? Our ancestors ate the manna in the wilderness; as it is written: 'He gave them bread from heaven to eat.'" Jesus said to them, "Very truly I tell you, it is not Moses who has given you the bread from heaven, but it is my Father who gives you the true bread from heaven. For the bread of God is the bread that comes down from heaven and gives life to the world." "Sir," they said, "always give us this bread." Then Jesus declared, "I am the bread of life. Whoever comes to me will never go hungry, and whoever believes in me will never be thirsty." (vv. 30-35)

Jesus is simply saying, "It is not about the bread. Stop worrying about the bread, for crying out loud. It is about what the bread points to. It is about God. I am the bread," he says. "So, all of that bread you ate yesterday, the manna in the wilderness, and all those miracles, they were all a means of revealing the glory of God. They were a means of drawing you nearer to me. They were intended to open your eyes to that which is standing before you: me."

"Behold," Jesus says, "this is the truth. I am the bread of heaven. I am the bread of life. If only you could see me for who

*This isn't a story about bread;
it is a story about God using
bread to meet his people.*

I am, then you would be filled, fulfilled, and never go hungry again."

The breaking of the bread is not intended to satisfy a physical hunger; it is intended to reveal God. He is the only one who has the power to satisfy the deepest longings of the human heart, our spiritual hunger. For so many people, Communion is troublesome and confusing because we focus so much on the tradition, the ritual, or the liturgy.

Whenever I strike up a conversation about Communion, inevitably someone begins talking about all the different ways in which Communion is received in different churches they have visited or of which they have been a part. Some churches serve the bread wafers. Others serve loaves of bread, matzo, or pita. Some denominations use wine or grape juice, while others use soda pop or even water. There are also all sorts of means and methods by which Communion is served and received. However we practice and refer to Communion though, the truth of the matter is that it is so much more than the food, the ritual, or the motions. Communion is about standing up, offering all you have in the act of joining others at the table, and then receiving all that God has to offer us. And what he offers us is much more than bread. It is mission. It is purpose. It is meaning. It is oneness. It is *communion*. And it can happen anywhere.

The amazing thing is that we can meet God and experience communion at any table as often as we want to. Communion is about us finding our seats at God's table so we might accept the grace of God that allows us to live fully into the future unafraid.

Throughout his lifetime, John Wesley suggested that we are to participate in the means of grace as often as possible.

The missional life carries the duty of constant communion. We are to travel down these ordinary roads that lead us to communion as often as possible. God commands us to "take and eat": in the same way we constantly obey God's commandment that "thou shall not kill," we should follow his command to "take and eat." The missional life should include breaking bread with others as often as possible, while remembering Christ each and every time. For whenever we do, Christ assures us that he is there. We break bread that we might see God.

We began this chapter by asking, *How do we carry the hope of Easter with us wherever we go?* We make every day like Easter by treating every table, every meal, as an opportunity to grow closer not only with the company we keep but also with God who reveals himself in the breaking of the bread.

Over the course of the last two years, Wendy and I have been intentional about inviting people over to share meals with us. We do not have the largest table in the world, but it works. Through countless numbers of meals we have made friends, shared life, and have grown closer to God. It is never about the bread. It is about growing closer with each other in love and growing closer to God. In the same way, through Holy Communion, Jesus Christ invites us to join him at his table that we might all find our seats and share a meal together.

The Lord's Table is a very intimate environment where everyone can gather, all are welcome, and the only thing required is that we come with an appetite. It doesn't matter who we are or where we are, what we've been through or what we're going through. We can always find common ground at the table because everyone at this table is in need of this meal. The Communion table is a table where people are encouraged

APPETITE

to have meaningful conversations about their life and faith. It's a table where people can become friends and churches begin to feel like family. It's a place where we can begin to experience authentic community and quality friendships. It is a place where we can meet God.

1. Jesus spent his last night breaking bread with his closest friends as well as with one who would betray him. Why do you think Jesus commanded us to give our enemy bread if he/she is hungry? Why is it important to share meals with other people?

2. The Latin word sacramentum (sacrament) means promise. What are the ways the Eucharist represents promise to you personally? How does God meet you in Holy Communion?

3. The author writes that all are welcome at the Lord's with the only requirement being an appetite. Do we have this sort of openness in the Church? What are the ways we exclude "outsiders" from partaking of God's grace?

Praying Always

And the word of the LORD came to him: "What are you
doing here, Elijah?" He replied, "I have been very zealous for
the LORD God Almighty. The Israelites have rejected your
covenant, torn down your altars, and put your prophets to
death with the sword. I am the only one left, and now they
are trying to kill me too." The LORD said, "Go out and stand
on the mountain in the presence of the LORD, for the LORD
is about to pass by." Then a great and powerful wind tore the
mountains apart and shattered the rocks before the LORD,
but the LORD was not in the wind. After the wind there was
an earthquake, but the LORD was not in the earthquake.
After the earthquake came a fire, but the LORD was not in
the fire. And after the fire came a gentle whisper. When
Elijah heard it, he pulled his cloak over his face and went out
and stood at the mouth of the cave.

—1 Kings 19:9-13

One of the more popular shows on TV these days is called *Glee*. It follows a group of eager and ambitious students (all members of a high school glee club) as they strive to outshine their singing competition while navigating the cruel halls of McKinley High School.

In one particular episode, the students talk about what it means to believe in God and to have faith—and they wonder what role prayer plays in all of it. Finn, a fairly faithless jock (and one of the main characters), is in the process of making a grilled cheese sandwich before heading out to football practice. Finn overcooks the sandwich only to discover the miraculous appearance of a burn mark that closely resembles the face of Jesus. He affectionately refers to his burned sandwich as "Grilled Cheesus."

The face of Jesus on this grilled cheese sandwich is so moving that it drives Finn to fall to his knees in prayer. The first thing he prays for is a football win. Next, he prays for a romantic encounter with his high school crush. He concludes his time of prayer focusing on the starting quarterback position. All three of Finn's prayer requests come to be, and so Finn continues to worship the Grilled Cheesus.

The reason I'm even mentioning this episode of *Glee* is because I think when most people think about prayer, we think just like Finn. When we think about abundant life or what it might take to pursue God, we often think in transactional terms—more possessions, more time, and more money. We believe that having more of these things will make us happy and that God will make it happen. God will give us more stuff. Therefore, we pray to God as though he were a genie. This is unfortunate, but this is how it works for most people.

As I've grown, my understanding of prayer has changed. James offers some descriptive instructions in the way of prayer. James tells us how to pray, how often to pray, what to pray for, and why we should even consider praying. Incidentally, his instructions look and feel a lot different from praying to Grilled Cheesus.

James 5:13-20 reads,

Is anyone among you in trouble? Let them pray. Is anyone happy? Let them sing songs of praise. Is anyone among you sick? Let them call the elders of the church to pray over them and anoint them with oil in the name of the Lord. And the prayer offered in faith will make the sick person well; the Lord will raise them up. If they have sinned, they will be forgiven. Therefore confess your sins to each other and pray for each other so that you may be healed. The prayer of a righteous person is powerful and effective. Elijah was a human being, even as we are. He prayed earnestly that it would not rain, and it did not rain on the land for three and a half years. Again he prayed, and the heavens gave rain, and the earth produced its crops. My brothers and sisters, if one of you should wander from the truth and someone should bring that person back, remember this: Whoever turns a sinner from the error of their way will save them from death and cover over a multitude of sins.

James is saying that we are to pray always and we are to pray fervently. No matter where we go, what we are doing, how we are feeling, we should pray always with passion and fervor. Therefore, when you suffer, go to God in prayer. When you're cheerful, sing songs of praise. When you sin, confess and pray for forgiveness. When you are sick, ask God to surround you, support you, intercede on your behalf, and you'll find salvation and healing.

The missional life is covered in prayer. It is grounded in an ongoing conversation with God, one that seeks to find God wherever we go and no matter what we are doing. Whenever we pray, whenever we speak, whenever we enter into this holy conversation, God is with us, faithfully listening and hearing all that we have to say. God hears our prayers no matter how poor our articulation. He hears us even when we ask for things for which we should not or need not ask.

People have a hard time praying like this, largely because we're hampered by the impression of God as a genie. We struggle with prayer because more times than not, we feel that we have not received what we've prayed for. This has been the story from the beginning of time. God doesn't always give us what we want; yet James tells his church (and all of us) that we are to pray fervently as a way of overcoming resistance and doubt. James points his parish to the past saying, "Elijah was a human being, even as we are. He prayed earnestly that it would not rain, and it did not rain on the land for three and a half years. Again he prayed, and the heavens gave rain, and the earth produced its crops" (vv. 17-18).

The Praying Man Hears

Elijah was a man who became a prophet of God. The name literally means "the Lord is my God," or "Yahweh is Lord." It was Elijah's ability to pray that has made him, in many minds, one of the greatest Old Testament prophets. Many people also believed that Elijah was the harbinger of the end of times. The Old Testament ends in Malachi 4:5-6 by referencing Elijah's hope-filled return. Malachi writes, listening

See, I will send the prophet Elijah to you before that great and dreadful day of the LORD comes. He will turn the hearts of the parents to their children, and the hearts of the children to their parents; or else I will come and strike the land with total destruction.

In the Gospels, Elijah's name is mentioned several times because people believed that Jesus was the second coming of Elijah rather than the Son of God. Elijah even made an appearance with Jesus on the Mount of Transfiguration as he stood beside Moses and the disciples.

But Elijah did not start his life with this kind of prominence. He started out like you and me. In 1 Kings 17, Elijah was hungry. He was thirsty. He wondered what he could do to have life and have it abundantly. Throughout much of his life, Elijah rarely spoke. He spent most of his time listening: it is through his story of listening and responding that we learn about the importance of prayer for the missional life.

Elijah teaches us that to pray is to listen and follow obediently even when the way is uncertain. In 1 Kings 17, the people of Israel have made it to the Promised Land. They have been settled there just long enough to have become corrupt, divided, and dysfunctional. In fact, by chapter 17, the king of Israel, King Ahab, has married a woman named Jezebel and not only begun worshiping Baal (another god) because of Jezebel's influence, but also begun to persecute and kill the prophets. Hundreds of prophets have been executed on account of Ahab and Jezebel.

It's at this point when Elijah, the prophet of the Lord, enters the scene. Elijah appears to the Israelites out of nowhere to relay a divine message. This whole time, as Ahab and Jezebel are corrupting Israel, Elijah is being nudged by God to leap to action.

Elijah appears before the most powerful couple in the world not knowing what will happen. Probably scared out of his mind, yet convinced by God that he needs to be there, he proclaims to Ahab, "Your spiritual barrenness will now be matched by agricultural barrenness and drought until you repent, fall to your knees, and become one with the Lord my God. Until you listen to the voice of God, until you pray, the drought will continue."

Prayer is holy conversation. It works just as any other conversation does. Someone speaks and someone listens. Prayer works both ways. God speaks and we listen. There are times when we speak and God listens. Most often than not, God calls us, speaks to us, and surrounds us. It's our job to look for God, listen to him, and respond. God leads and we follow.

God speaks to Elijah. He leads him to go and speak with the king of Israel, the most powerful person in the world, and Elijah responds to God by living, acting, and ultimately speaking in accordance with God's voice. God speaks, and Elijah listens and responds. This is prayer.

Obedience Has a Cover Letter

I was in fifth grade the first time I remember hearing God speak to me. I was sitting near a boy named Steven. He was the boy that other boys picked on. My family lived near Steven's family in Detroit. I was one of the few who knew what it was like to live in Steven's house. His parents were separated, and his life wasn't easy.

Steven was struggling with math. Every now and then our teacher would call on him to solve problems aloud. One day she called on him and it happened to be a moment when Steven couldn't focus and couldn't give the right answer. Rather than coaching him through the problem or letting him pass, our teacher actually called him names. She called him "stupid," then "lazy," and finally a "nerd."

I didn't say anything at that moment, figuring that if I did, she would call me names as well. I remember walking home from school that day, knowing that God was nudging me to do something. He was saying to me, "Scott, you have to do something about this. You have to speak to your teacher about what happened. Tell her that she can no longer teach fifth grade. Tell her it is not okay to treat students this way, especially Steven."

After school that day, I drafted a newspaper article (an editorial) that described what happened in class that day. In it I pleaded with my teacher to apologize for what she had said to Steven and for her conduct in the class. I put a cover letter on it, walked it back over to the school, and dropped one copy in the school library, another one in the principal's office, and then I was going to deliver a copy to her classroom as well. When I reached my teacher's classroom, my heart sank! There she was still sitting at her desk.

I had come face-to-face with the most powerful woman in my fifth grade world. This was the moment of truth. What was going to happen? Was listening to this stirring, this divine calling, really worth it? I wondered if I was even doing the right thing.

There is some uncertainty whenever we pray. Listening to God's voice does not always make it easier to know if what we are doing is actually in accordance with God's will. Praying is listening for God's voice and then doing our best to respond to what we believe God is urging us to do. It's about being obedient even in the midst of uncertainty. It requires steadfast patience and at times perseverance.

Elijah's story teaches us that to pray is to respond to God's call even when the way is uncertain and that when we do, great things will happen. Elijah had to address the king of Israel, the most powerful man in the world, and deliver some horrible news. I only had to address my fifth grade teacher, but let me tell you, the result was pretty incredible.

My teacher was shocked when I showed up in her classroom. I handed her the editorial and said, "I've also copied the principal and *Paw Prints* (the school newspaper). I want you to know that what you did was unacceptable." I can still remember her look of disbelief, but she apologized. She changed the way she addressed her students, we became great friends, and Steven ended up going on to have great academic success.

To pray is also to be alert. We must turn on our radar and work to detect the presence of God all around us. Can you imagine standing up to the most powerful man in the world as Elijah did? Can you imagine mustering up the necessary confidence and courage to tell him that God isn't going to let it rain on his land anymore? How do you think you would feel? Elijah was probably terrified, but he pressed forward in faith. He followed through. He lived fully, putting one foot in front of the next according to God's voice, and he quickly discovered that God had more to say.

The Praying Man Sees

God is always with us. The name Emmanuel literally means "God with us." Our God says that he will never let us go, and such was the case for Elijah. After he tells the king of

I had come
face-to-face
with the most
powerful woman
in my
fifth grade world.
This was the
moment of truth.

Israel that it won't rain for three years, God instructs Elijah to run like crazy in the opposite direction. Elijah does a great and audacious deed in response to God's nudging. He acts obediently and then he is asked to escape into the wilderness without food or water. God tells him, "Go from here and turn eastward, and hide yourself by the Wadi Cherith, which is east of the Jordan" (1 Kings 17:3, NRSV).

Elijah's response must have been, "Wait, what? Seriously? You just sent me to tell the most powerful man in the world that the water is going to run out, and I actually did it! Now you want me to run away without any food or drink, and by the way, God, there is no more water. What kind of deal is this? You're making me look like a coward and a fool, not to mention, I'm probably going to starve in the wilderness. I thought after doing all of this you would set me up with a comfortable retirement, not send me to starve!"

But Elijah escapes anyway. He continues to listen to and follow God's instruction faithfully. This is what a life of prayer looks like. This is pursuing God. For three years, Elijah wanders without provision throughout the wilderness in the midst of one of the most severe droughts in Israel's history.

One might think Elijah would become ill or depressed or angry. Yet the opposite happens. In the wilderness, Elijah's radar turns fully on! He becomes more alert than ever. He sees God everywhere. He sees God first by a river, when what appear to be angels drop him food from the sky. He senses God in the birds as he watches ravens (the nastiest of birds) deliver him gifts of meat and bread. He even hears the voice of God and decides to follow what he hears to meet a starving widow who also has the ability to feed him. He sees God in her and in her son. He befriends the widow, and God actually uses him to resurrect her son.

During these three years Elijah demonstrates that to pray is also to be alert. It is to look for God, to put up our radar that we might detect the presence of God all around us—in the birds, in our neighbors, in our encounters, and all along the journey.

Where do you sense the presence of God in the midst of your journey? Are you looking diligently for God? Is your radar finely tuned?

The Praying Man's Mission

After three years of drought and famine pass, Elijah is given a new command by God. In the interim, he has been filled with provisions, filled with the Spirit, and living off of his faith in God. He is commanded to return to the land from which he fled. His divine orders are to meet up with King Ahab and Queen Jezebel, the royal couple, only this time he isn't a nameless prophet. Everyone knows who he is.

Elijah confronts the couple immediately:

"I have not made trouble for Israel," Elijah replied. "But you and your father's family have. You have abandoned the LORD's commands and have followed the Baals. Now summon the people from all over Israel to meet me on Mount Carmel. And bring the four hundred and fifty prophets of Baal and the four hundred prophets of Asherah, who eat at Jezebel's table." (1 Kings 18:18-19)

Ahab and Jezebel have corrupted the land of Israel. They are worshiping false idols. They are killing God's children. Even though they are in the middle of one of the greatest droughts in history, they are hoarding food and starving the masses.

So, the great showdown is set. Elijah, the prophet of the Lord, against 450 prophets of Baal. Elijah says,

> "Get two bulls for us. Let Baal's prophets choose one for themselves, and let them cut it into pieces and put it on the wood but not set fire to it. I will prepare the other bull and put it on the wood but not set fire to it. Then you call on the name of your god, and I will call on the name of the LORD. The god who answers by fire—he is God." Then all the people said, "What you say is good." (Vv. 23-24)

So the hungry and desperate onlookers place two altars out in a field and lay two lifeless bulls on those altars. Elijah steps to the side, allowing the prophets of Baal to summon their god first.

All 450 prophets begin crying out and calling on the name of Baal, shouting, "Baal, answer us!" (v. 26). There is no voice and no answer. They limp about the altar and call for Baal all day long. After eight straight hours of calling for their god without any answer, Elijah asks people to gather around his altar. "Come here to me," he says, and folks gather around the prophet (v. 30).

First, he prepares the altar of the LORD that has been thrown down. He places some stones on it, digs a trench around it, and pours water on the whole thing until it is dripping wet. Then he begins to pray:

> LORD, the God of Abraham, Isaac and Israel, let it be known today that you are God in Israel and that I am your servant and have done all these things at your command. Answer me, LORD, answer me, so these people will know that you, LORD, are God, and that you are turning their hearts back again. (Vv. 36-37)

God answers Elijah, and the fire of the LORD falls and consumes the burnt offering, the wood, the stones, and the dust, and it even licks up the water that is in the trench. "When all the people saw this, they fell prostrate and cried, 'The LORD—he is God! The LORD—he is God!'" (v. 39).

While Elijah celebrates and rejoices, Queen Jezebel is still not convinced of God's power. Within a few hours, she sends Elijah a message. In it Jezebel vows to kill him as she has so many other prophets. Elijah flees immediately as he did before, only this time the Holy Spirit does not drive him there; his fear does. Jezebel's threats terrify Elijah, but what frightens him more is that he can't hear God anymore. Elijah can't hear anything. His radar stops working. At one point he feels so alone that he can't bear another step. He quickly finds shelter under a shady tree, lays down beside it, and asks God to let him die right there. He says to God, "I've had enough of this."

After Fire

Have you ever felt that way? Stuck in life? Mired and paralyzed by fear? Without any direction? That things used to be going so well, but now there is just darkness?

Maybe it was the game of chicken with the prophets of Baal that did it to him. Maybe Elijah felt as though he was so powerful that he didn't really need God. Perhaps Elijah forgot that God was responsible for all that had been happening in his life. Sometimes when we get exactly what we want, there can be a terrible vacuum afterward. Sometimes when we get what we want, we stop praying, we stop needing God. We believe that we don't need God anymore. These are the moments when it seems as if all the energy that had enabled us to reach our goals has gone away. Where did it all go? Have

The prophet of the Lord against 450 prophets of Baal

you ever felt that you used to be so motivated, and now you're stuck, tired, and without a clue as to what comes next?

Maybe Elijah was physically and mentally exhausted. Sometimes deep conversations take their toll. Intense connections cannot go on forever. Elijah was listening and responding faithfully without hesitation for several years. Things continued to happen to Elijah, one thing after another. There had been no time to rest. Maybe Elijah was simply tired.

Or maybe Elijah was tired of being a prophet. Maybe he said, "With all due respect, God, I'm too tired to continue. You're going to have to call someone else to take my place, because I don't have anything left."

For whatever reason, Elijah had had enough of it. So in his darkest moment, Elijah asked God to take his life. He laid down under a broom tree and went to sleep.

But then Elijah heard a bunch of racket.

A wind blew so hard around him that it was breaking stones. Then an earthquake hit. The ground around him started to tremble. Then came fire. Heat and light danced all around him. And then after all of that commotion, the void of total silence followed. And the silence had a sound all its own.

When Elijah registered the silence, he wrapped his face in his cloak and finally stood up. The voice of God whispered to him a question: "What are you doing here, Elijah?" (1 Kings 19:13).

Elijah replied, fully awake now, saying, "Surely the Lord is in this place."

Living fully is about waking up to the presence of God all around us, even in the stillness, even in the darkness. Prayer requires that we wake up and attempt to sense God around us.

Have you ever run into people who are talking about an event or a time or place when they were just going about their everyday business when the Holy Spirit showed up?

"I was praying with my neighbor the other day, and *then the Holy Spirit showed up . . .*"

"I was at church the other day in worship, *and then the Holy Spirit showed up . . .*"

Anecdotes like that have never made much sense to me. I wonder what Elijah would have said if he could have described the situation he was in, "The wind was blowing, the earth was trembling, there was fire all over the place, *and then God showed up . . .*"

Do you think that's really the way it happened? Did God wait to show up until after the wind, earthquake, and fire had passed? Or did it take that long for Elijah to simply wake up?

Jacob, another Old Testament figure, met God shortly after waking up as well. On the run in the wilderness, catching a moment's respite, Jacob was lying with his head on a rock when he saw visions of the Lord ascending and descending. Then he woke up saying, "Surely the LORD is in this place" (Genesis 28:16). Was it that the Lord had finally arrived, or was it that Jacob woke up? Part of what it means to pray is to wake up to the presence of God that is all around us, everywhere we go.

When we read the story of Elijah, we don't get to hear much from him vocally. Instead, we learn that prayer is all about listening, searching, and following or responding to a call. This aspect of prayer might seem odd to us, but that's largely the case because most of us continue to view prayer as Finn praying to his "Grilled Cheesus." We pray when we want or need something and stop when we're done asking for it. We never consider that we have a responsibility, even an obligation, to listen.

Elijah shows us something totally different. Elijah listened, looked, and constantly searched for the voice of the Lord. Prayer is a way of life. It is an ongoing and holy conversation filled with sights, sounds, whispers, and nudges that we might not hear God if we don't stop to listen. God is always working, always speaking, always sending us things like burning bushes and blowing winds; he can even intervene in and through our grilled cheeses.

Jesus tells Israel and all those who followed him that, "My Father is always working, and so am I" (John 5:17, NLT). Our responsibility is to *wake up* to the presence and voice of God. This is the aim of the missional life. Missional living is waking up to the presence of God and responding to God's presence in a way that brings about a life rooted in holy conversation. It is praying always, seeking always, listening always in thought, word, and deed so that every movement is in step with God's mission of perfect communion—reconciling us with each other and with God.

and the silence had a sound all its own

1. If prayer is about an ongoing conversation with God, how often are you on the hearing side? What are ways you may become more of a listener in your personal prayer life?

2. We are often prone to view suffering as God's punishment, but it is in the wilderness that Elijah most clearly sees God. What might this tell us about God's favor and nearness during hard times in our lives? Recount times when God was near and faithful to you in a difficult season.

3. Much of prayer is just getting in on what God is already doing and hearing a prayer that the Lord is already making on our behalf. Ask the Lord to reveal to you what he is up to in your life and the lives of those around you; then ask him how you may get in on it.

Spending Less and Giving More

We've talked about Holy Communion, we've talked about community, we've talked about worship and reading Scripture, and we have even talked about prayer. By now you are probably wondering, "When is this going to end?" If you are thinking this, then it is my cue to interrupt your thought process.

"And just when you thought it was all over . . ."

If you're a baseball fan, you've probably heard this phrase at the bottom of the ninth inning. Imagine (or recount) this scenario: your team is trailing by a few runs and the game is all but over. Yet somehow your team has loaded the bases. The crowd starts to roar as your cleanup hitter steps up to the plate. It is in the midst of a fan frenzy that the announcer finally rises above the noise of the crowd to shout, "And just when you thought it was all over!"

If you are not a sports fan, perhaps you heard this phrase in the fall of 2000. At two in the morning in early November the United States was electing a new president. Earlier that night the polling stations had indicated that Al Gore was going to be the clear winner. In the early morning hours, however, the tide began to turn. Votes kept coming in. At around 2:00 a.m., newscasters all over the country were saying some variation of, "And just when you thought it was over!"

Perhaps politics isn't really your thing either. In that case, you might have heard this phrase uttered about New Orleans as Katrina's clouds finally cleared. The winds finally died down, the rain had ceased, all the damage had been done as far as everyone could tell. But then we watched the horrible scene unfold: over twenty thousand individuals were stranded with nowhere to go, nothing to drink, and no one to help them. Riots, looting, and long lines of hungry people materialized in just a few hours, while we wondered, "What do we do?"

Looking at our TVs in stunned silence, we thought quietly to ourselves, *And just when we thought it was all over.*

Life has a way of doing that sometimes. Whenever we think we have things pegged, pinned down, or accounted for, they change. My wife and I had something like that happen to us not long ago. We finally had good financial footing. Our real-life budget finally resembled the one we put on paper. In addition to our finances, our workout schedules were manageable, our church calendars were coordinated, our spiritual lives were beginning to flow together, and our parsonage was beginning to feel like home. We had settled into a comfortable routine, so we planned a vacation to visit Wendy's family on their farm in Louisiana. We were finally ready to relax a little. Things were under control.

We had been there for less than twenty-four hours when we heard the phone ring. It was eleven o'clock at night. The voice (the Michigan police) on the other end of the line informed Wendy, "There's been a break-in." Wendy looked at me with fearful tears in her eyes and said, "Just when we thought it was all over."

Have you ever experienced this?

The Young Professional

In Matthew 19 (paraphrased), Jesus meets a rich young ruler (or young professional, as I like to say). The young professional approaches Jesus on the road heading toward Jerusalem. "Teacher," he asks, "what good deed must I do to have eternal life?"

Jesus replies, "Why do you ask me about these things? There is only one who is good. If you wish to live fully, keep the commandments."

This is extravagance:

the God of the world

humbling himself.

The young man replies, "Are you talking about the Ten Commandments, Jesus? No murdering, adultery, stealing, lying? Those commandments?"

"Yes, I am."

"Good, because I have all of those covered. I have kept all of those commandments. So, what do I still lack?"

It is at this point in the dialogue that I always wonder what the young professional is hoping to hear. Is he hoping to hear that he is in full compliance? That he is good to go and his ticket to heaven is waiting for him at the will-call window? That he is as good as Jesus? If so, he does not hear anything of the sort.

Jesus says to him, "If you wish to live fully, go, sell all of your possessions, give the money to the poor, and then you may come and follow me."

And just when the young professional thought it was all over, he suddenly had a long way to go.

I do not know about you, but this happens to me all the time. Whenever I think everything is in order or whenever I think I have it all together, the other shoe inevitably drops. In this passage Jesus lowers the boom on this unsuspecting man who seems to have everything under control, saying, "If you wish to be my disciple, if you want to follow me, if you desire to pursue God, then you must sell everything you own."

Really?

Yes, really.

For those of you who are hoping this passage does not apply to you, somehow, it gets worse. Immediately following this passage, Jesus tells his disciples (and all of us) that it is indeed harder for the rich to inherit eternal life than it is for a camel to pass through the eye of a needle.

Seriously?

Yes, seriously.

This passage has been one of the toughest passages for me to swallow, even ten years after leaving my career in investments. Jesus, the Son of God, demands extravagant generosity of the young professional. He demands financial sacrifice. So, how are we to interpret this passage? Do we take it seriously? Where do we go with God's instruction for extravagant generosity?

There is something extremely challenging about being confronted with extravagant generosity. Have you ever received a gift you did not deserve? A gift that cost too much or a gift given to you by someone you tend to disregard? Undeserved gifts or sacrificial gifts are hard to handle, but as difficult as they might be to receive, they are even more challenging to hand out (especially when we're talking in terms of sacrifice.) That being said, I believe extravagant generosity to be a central dimension to the missional life and our ability to live fully.

Extravagant generosity is at the root of God's love. John 3:16 tells us that "God so loved the world that he gave his only Son, that whoever believes in him shall not perish but have eternal life." This is extravagance: The God of the world humbling himself.

I did not embody extravagant generosity when I was a young man. I was not a churchgoer. I am not even sure I was a Christian. I did some good things, but Jesus and I were not friends. To be honest, I did not buy into God's story. Sacrificial love, extravagant generosity, amazing grace? I needed a little more control over my life than that.

I had a picture in my mind's eye of what I wanted to be when I grew up, and that picture didn't include giving it all away. I was too driven. At eighteen, I began working for my first investment company, and by the age of twenty-one I had become a partner at a small financial planning group. My mission was not to live fully; it was to make it to Wall Street. Needless to say, practicing sacrificial love or living a life filled with extravagant generosity was not a part of the plan.

During that time, I attended church only reluctantly. I talked about it from time to time and thought about it sporadically, but I never lived it or understood it. Unlike the young professional in Matthew 19, it would not have even crossed my mind to approach Jesus to ask him what I needed to do in order to find life. But in 2003 after a series of God-inspired events involving a church van, a great connection with the pastor of my home church, and a younger sister who was leading me spiritually, I ended up leaving everything I knew—a career, a city, and a life filled with excess—in order to attend seminary.

Off the Map

I enrolled at Duke Divinity School unsure of what I was going to do. I guess I had visions of streamlining stewardship campaigns, building endowments, or revising the investment policies of large congregations. Back then my favorite Scripture passage about money was the parable of the talents. Unlike the story of the rich young ruler, this was a story about a God who blesses people for their investment expertise. Even the people who returned to God having earned simple interest were rewarded eternally. That was my kind of story. I thought, *I can totally do this.* So I headed to seminary hoping to employ my skill set for the good of the church and make a great living in the process. It sounded like a good plan to me, and it would have been had I not been so intent on making money.

Jesus says, "No one can serve two masters. Either you will hate the one and love the other, or you will be devoted to the one and despise the other. You cannot serve both God and money" (Matthew 6:24). The truth of the matter is this: I was still in love with money as I headed off to seminary. I was not willing to let go of my interest in and love for finding, accumulating, and creating wealth. Yet Jesus said clearly, "No one can serve two masters."

Any hopes I had of hanging on to my former life in finance were dashed when I received my first church assignment. In the summer of 2004 I packed my bags, loaded up my car, and headed to a small country church in the mountains of North Carolina. It was a far cry from Wall Street.

Dana United Methodist Church was a one-hundred-year-old church of fifty people, with an average age of seventy-five. They were looking for someone young and gifted to lead them. Dana, North Carolina, wasn't on any map. There was one red light, one post office, and one supermarket, and it seemed that the combined number of cattle and apple farms outpaced the population.

When my supervisor told me this was where I was headed, I protested. I said, "Don't you know who you're talking to? I'm from Detroit, the Motor City. I'm your money guy! Surely there's a church out there that can use my gifts. Surely there's a congregation in need of a financial overhaul or some sort of investment help. Isn't there a church that needs to raise some capital? That's where I belong."

Wall Street

I protested until finally my supervisor stopped me and calmly reminded me, "Scott, this isn't up to you. This is in God's hands now. It's out of your control. You're going to Dana, North Carolina, and I promise that you'll find what you're looking for there." When it became clear that he wasn't going to budge, I thought about backing out of divinity school altogether. But eventually, reluctantly, I went. I traveled to Dana, North Carolina.

I arrived on a Saturday afternoon. I spent a little time driving around the town until I made it to my summer residence. Winding through the mountain gaps, I drove down into one of the valleys where I discovered that I would be living in a single-wide trailer for the summer. It was silver and brown and positioned right next to a fairly large cattle farm. There was no TV, radio, or cell reception. Instead, they had a landline that wasn't able to make outgoing phone calls and only received them when the electric cattle fence was turned off. It was a far cry from Manhattan.

During that summer, the attendance of the Dana church doubled. We built a youth group, we repaired several houses, and I made some lifelong friends. But what continues to stick with me most clearly are the memories of my first pastoral visit.

More Like Wringing Chickens' Necks

Within a few days of being there, I made my first pastoral visit with a ninety-nine-year-old woman named Dolly, who I affectionately refer to as my first victim. Dolly lived in an old house behind the church. Her home was in complete disrepair. There were mattresses in the windows, the wood siding was rotting away, and the roof was more tarp than shingle. The front porch was sagging badly, though it still managed to support two rocking chairs, which was where Dolly spent most of her time.

I remember driving up to her house in my red Pontiac. My windows were down, the sunroof was open, and my music was blaring. As I pulled up her gravel driveway, I remember seeing chickens running around everywhere. I had no idea what I was going to say to her, and I didn't know what she was looking for from me. I certainly didn't know what I was doing, but one thing was for certain: I couldn't figure out what all these chickens were doing running around. Why would anyone have so many chickens? This whole scene was very confusing to me. Detroit deals in steel, not poultry. As I got out of my car, trying to give a good first impression as the new pastor, I said the only thing I could think of at the time. I asked Dolly, "What are all these chickens doing here?"

She replied, "Well, I gotta eat something."

I navigated the rickety porch steps and sat down next to her. Together we rocked in our chairs. As we chatted, she made fun of me for being a Yankee and shared stories with me about how her town had changed over her lifetime. I never got a word in. I just listened to her talk. After about forty-five minutes, still having said nothing profound or enlightening, I felt as if I were failing on my first pastoral visit. So I asked if I could read some Scripture and pray with her before I left. She said, "Sure." So I did, and then I got up to say good-bye.

As I stood up, Dolly stood with me and said, "Hold on, hold on! Before you go, I want to give you something—a gift."

I protested, "No, no. Dolly, you don't have to give me anything. Just invite me back and that'll be plenty for me."

Dolly walked to the edge of her front porch and reached into her apron pockets. When she got to the edge, she bent over and pulled her hands from her pockets. As she did, the chickens ran toward her as if she had something in her pockets for them to eat. And as they came closer, she opened her hands as though to feed them, but I noticed that her hands were empty. I didn't have time to think about it or ask why because one of the chickens had gotten close enough that Dolly could actually reach out and grab it. And that is exactly what she did. In one quick motion she grabbed the bird, wrung its neck, and handed the still-twitching bird to me.

"Oh my! Well . . . thank you, Dolly. You (really, really) shouldn't have!" I grabbed the chicken by its feet, walked over to my car, laid it in the trunk, and took off as fast as I could.

The more I thought about my conversation with Dolly, the more I came to realize that this was the first time I ever really encountered God's extravagant generosity. It just took me some time to see it clearly.

Dolly showed me how to give sacrificially. In one swift motion, she demonstrated real power. She gave me an undeserved gift, and I had to receive it. As she handed me the dead chicken, she shared with me the grace of God—Christian community. I thought to myself, *This was Christ on the cross kind of stuff. This was Jesus standing on trial. This was giving more even when there was nothing more to give. This was turning an implement of death into a sign of life.*

In one gesture, Dolly introduced me to the life, death, and resurrection of Jesus Christ. I discovered the gospel and the power of God's extravagant generosity. Here was a woman who had nothing, yet was willing to give me, a total stranger, part of what she counted on for sustenance.

Dolly had no fear. She was joyful, exuberant, and confident. As I drove away from her house, and after I got past the shock of it all, for the first time in my life I realized why I am here and why I was created.

Dolly taught me that life begins when we realize that there is plenty we can still do even when we don't have much to offer. She taught me that living a missional life begins when, like Jesus, we extend ourselves with joy and thanksgiving. When we give sacrificially, we find what we are looking for because we join God in the mighty acts of Jesus Christ. When we offer all that we have and all that we are, we find the peace of Christ that surpasses all understanding.

Offerings, First Fruits, Fat Portions

The middle-aged couple asks their financial adviser, "What must we save so that we can retire comfortably?" High school students ask their guidance counselors, "What classes and what grades do I need so I have a shot at a prestigious college and can ultimately get a great job earning lots of money?" The patient sitting across from her doctor asks, "What can we do so I can spend more time on earth with my children?" We all want to know what we need to do in order to have life and have it abundantly. For many, finding peace or living fully is attached to earthly things—our possessions and our riches. In recent years, I've realized that finding God's peace looks more like wringing chickens' necks than it does investing in stock portfolios. It looks more like giving it all away as opposed to accumulating more stuff.

Living missionally means we strive for the day when we become not only the recipients of God's perfect love but also distributors of it. It means we don't simply claim God, accept

better to give [poultry]
than to receive

Jesus Christ, or attend church regularly or reluctantly. Living missionally means that we are able to sell everything we have, laying it all aside, in willingness to do whatever it takes to share God's love with those around us.

The young professional asks Jesus, "What good deeds must I do in order to follow you perfectly? What must I do to have life abundantly?"

Jesus says to him, "Go and sell everything you own, give it to the poor, and then follow me."

Maybe you are thinking, *I can hardly crack open the Bible, let alone make it to church. How can it be that I would ever get to a place where I could actually go and sell all that I own?*

Note that Jesus is not necessarily talking to us in this passage. He is asking the rich young ruler, who is blameless in the eyes of the law, to sell all he has because it's the one area of his life that still separates him from God. Riches, power, and possessions are impeding the man's ability to follow God, and you can see this by the way he responds to Jesus' command—with grief and despair.

Can you imagine the depth of pain he was feeling? This rich young ruler was face-to-face with the God he loved enough to faithfully follow all of his commandments. This faithful young professional was staring into the perfect eyes of God, having a conversation about eternal life. But when he was asked by God to leave it all behind, to sell all of his possessions for a taste of perfection and oneness, he could not do it.

Why not? For fear of losing his first love—money and all that money can buy. God desires our love more than anything else. God is extravagantly generous: he gives us the undeserved gift of mercy and grace. God loves us so much and wants so desperately for us to love him in return that he actually sent his only Son, Jesus Christ, fully human and fully divine, to live perfectly and then die sacrificially so that we might one day become perfect in love like him.

One of the ways we experience that love is by giving away all that we've been given. This happens when we offer our lives, our hearts, our minds, and eventually our belongings up to God's pleasure and divine disposal.

Some of the earliest descriptions of worship in the Bible—starting in Genesis 4 and throughout the Torah—did not involve singing. They did not involve preaching. They involved offering. In Genesis 4, we see Cain and Abel worshiping:

> Now Abel kept flocks, and Cain worked the soil. In the course of time Cain brought some of the fruits of the soil as an offering to the LORD. And Abel also brought an offering—fat portions from some of the firstborn of his flock. The LORD looked with favor on Abel and his offering. (Vv. 2-4)

Worship for them was most clearly seen in presenting God with an offering. Without being taught, without standing before God face-to-face, both Cain and Abel knew that pursuing God included offering a portion of the fruit of their labors.

This practice continues throughout Scripture. In Genesis 8, after Noah got off the ark, he built an altar and offered God a sacrifice. When Abraham sought to love and honor God, he built an altar and offered a sacrifice. So, too, did Abraham's son, Isaac, and his grandson, Jacob. While we no longer offer the same sacrifices, even today, pursuing God requires that we offer all that we are and all that we have to him. Our gifts, what we offer to God, are expressions of our gratitude and love.

This is why the ways in which we treat our money matter. Our offerings, how we spend our money, and the measure with which we give are not only acts of worship but also ways in which we can grow deeper in love with God.

The writer of Proverbs says, "Honor the LORD with your wealth, with the firstfruits of all your crops; then your barns will be filled to overflowing, and your vats will brim over with new wine" (3:9-10). Those who freely give all that they've been given often find themselves to be the recipients of many more blessings.

Surprisingly, this is a consistent teaching in the Scriptures. Proverbs 11:24-25 says, "One person gives freely, yet gains even more; another withholds unduly, but comes to poverty. A generous person will prosper; whoever refreshes others will be refreshed."

This scripture is about generosity not only toward God but also toward others. And there are dozens of proverbs like this one. Even though it's taken me a long time, I have finally discovered this: blessings come from extravagant generosity.

God's Country

As a young man in my early twenties, I was never willing to give God the firstfruits of my life. I did not tithe because I did not understand why I should. I was committing my time, and I was praying. I was living, loving, and volunteering for the church. I was even able to sacrifice a sizable income in order to head off to seminary to pursue a theological education. For some reason, though, I could not bring myself to tithe. Then, in a series of months, I met two boys, each living in separate parts of the country. One lived in the heart of Kansas City; the other lived in the mountains of Kentucky.

The first boy was named Bubby. He was a normal seven-year-old, born and raised in Hazard County, Kentucky. I got to spend time in "God's country" while serving alongside several people who felt called to make homes safe, dry, and warm for those who were cold, alone, and wandering in the darkness. I can still remember meeting Bubby and his family on the first night of my church's mission trip. I can't recall his parents' names, but I'll never forget Bubby! He was an incredible little man.

Bubby loved adventure. He loved animals. He loved wrestling with his dogs, hunting for snakes, and doing all the things adventurous seven-year-olds do. My work team and I adored Bubby. He was such a joy to be around, so we always invited him to eat lunch with us or take breaks with us, work on the roof with us, or do whatever it was we were up to. He would welcome us in the morning and say good-bye to us in the evening. He was our little buddy.

The week was going well until Thursday morning. When we arrived, Bubby was standing in our parking spot, ready to go. He was unusually excited, and before we could get out of the van, he shouted, "Hi, guys! Today's my birthday!" So we all shouted, "Happy Birthday, Bubby!" However, we were all a bit sad because we didn't have anything for him. We had no idea it was his birthday, and we knew that Bubby, just like any other seven-year-old, was excited to receive presents.

He stuck around us all day. We couldn't shake him. At lunch, we tried to make him feel special: we pooled our food together to give him an extra cookie and an extra bag of chips, but that was all that we could manage. We hadn't known it was his birthday, but it was still difficult for us that

DIVINE DISPOSAL

we didn't have a gift for him. We suspected, given his outward appearance, that we were his only hope for presents.

We made it through the day. Bubby had to run inside to fetch something, so we quickly packed up our things for the day and started to load into the vans. We hoped we could avoid the inevitable, but Bubby came running out of his home toward the van yelling, "Wait, wait, wait! Guys, what about my birthday presents?"

All eyes turned to me. I mustered up the courage, begrudgingly exited the van, and approached Bubby with my hat in my hands. "I'm sorry, Bubby, but we didn't have time to get you any presents today."

Rather than being dejected, Bubby looked confused. He just stood there looking at me quizzically. After a moment he said, "No, I have birthday presents for each of you." Out of his pocket he pulled eight pocketknives, each of which he had found walking to and from the drugstore located about a mile down the road. He announced, "I found one for each of you."

Bubby wanted to give us gifts for his birthday. Bubby's family didn't have anything to give, yet Bubby gave all that he had to us on a day when we were supposed to be giving thanks for him. My friends, that's *agape*. Bubby's generosity was sacrificial love. Bubby had real power. Bubby was living fully whether or not he knew it. This is what the missional life looks like.

• • •

A few months later I met another boy named Javon. He lived much closer to my home in downtown Kansas City. I met Javon through an experience I had with members of my church at Resurrection Downtown. Our church is located in the heart of Kansas City. We are a very diverse group of people, most of whom are nominally religious or nonreligious. One Monday morning after attending a worship gathering the previous Sunday, a member of our church (and a fourth grade teacher in one of the poorest elementary schools in Kansas City) went to work. But this particular Monday was different from most. This teacher was so inspired by the worship service from the night before that he was still singing the songs. He walked into class singing, and after only a few measures Javon, one of his fourth grade students, overheard him.

"What are you singing?" Javon asked his teacher. Javon didn't have much. He was on the free lunch program. These were the only hot meals he ate. Javon scrounged around for school supplies and wore hand-me-down clothing. Rarely did he have access to full meals over the weekend.

The teacher answered awkwardly, "Oh, just a couple songs we sang in church yesterday."

Javon replied, "You go to church?"

"Yeah, I go to Resurrection Downtown," said the teacher.

"What's it like?"

"It's hot. We don't have any air conditioning," the teacher described, "so it's really hot in church, sometimes over one hundred degrees."

"That's not right! You don't have any air conditioning? You gotta have air-conditioning!"

Javon had been sitting at his desk for just a few minutes, but after thinking about his teacher worshiping in the heat, he walked back up to his teacher's desk. He asked him if it would be all right if he made him a fan. The teacher was shocked and flattered. He said, "Absolutely!"

Javon began cutting semicircles out of construction paper. He wrote inspirational messages on them such as, "Think cool thoughts" or "Imagine you're an Eskimo." He drew pictures of the beach and pictures of ice cubes and igloos. He even drew a picture of the cross. By the time he had finished, all of his classmates had witnessed and wondered what he was doing. After he showed them the finished products, they joined him. Javon's classmates started making their own fans to give away as well. It took them about an hour to cut and complete their fans. Once they had all finished, Javon took them to the library to get them laminated. He then glued on popsicle sticks as handles, and by the end of the day, the fourth grade class had made over seventy-five hand fans for our church.

Javon was a boy who had no connection to our church. He had nothing to his name. No lunch to eat. No money. No resources. No support network. Nothing at all. Yet he was moved by compassion. He collected his friends, he organized them, and he had them all cut out hand fans so that his teacher didn't have to sweat in church.

Buddy and Javon, one from the mountains of Kentucky and the other from the urban core of Kansas City, were willing to give me everything they had though they had nothing. Then how much more should I be willing to give? Jesus said, "Go, sell your possessions" (Matthew 19:21).

Generosity that Transforms

When Christ died, we became the recipients of the grace his death purchased for us. This was his free gift. God's extravagant generosity should move us and enable us to do all things. God's perfect love enables us to do all things on the path toward abundant life, or what the young professional calls eternal life. God's grace moves us to go and do likewise.

I've discovered that living sacrificially doesn't always happen at once. God doesn't generally meet us where we are and tell us to leave everything we have to follow him. It's usually a much slower process. What ends up happening is that God meets us and leads us into a church, a worship service, or some similar kind of situation. Sometimes this happens because of the persistence of a parent or the gentle nudging of a spouse. Perhaps friends invite us to join them. Or maybe it's a ninety-nine-year-old woman, a child like Bubby, or a fourth grader like Javon.

Whatever your story is, something or someone moved you to go deeper, to pursue God, to search for meaning, and because of this encounter you were changed. Your life was transformed, even if in a small way. Your desire to be involved in spiritual things increased. So you started reading Scripture, began to pray, or maybe felt as though you worshiped for the very first time. Eventually, you made a promise to God, so you began contributing your time. Then came your money.

You started out by making a donation to mission projects; after a while you realized that the church also needed your financial assistance, so you helped out by giving in proportion of your income. After a while, perhaps giving money wasn't enough. You visited a soup kitchen or volunteered to work on some dilapidated homes.

All the while your love of God has been intensifying, your relationship with Christ increasing, and upon looking back, you realize that more and more of your life is dedicated to the love of God and the love of neighbor. Just like that you discover that your mind is engaged, your body is at work, your

No one can serve two masters. Either you will hate the one and love the other, or you will be devoted to the one and despise the other. You cannot serve both God and money.

Matthew 6:24

soul is filling with God's grace, and your Spirit is growing with love for God. Your life is being transformed from one that is set on power, prestige, and material things into one committed to running a race that begins and ends with God.

Giving extravagantly is a lot to ask of anyone. *Sell all of your things.* It is just short of unimaginable. The Lord says to us, *Give me everything you have.* Living missionally means we live with the understanding that the Christian faith calls each and every one of us into an extraordinary life. A life that looks and acts different from anything we've ever seen.

Most of us, when we take the time to really look at our-selves critically, see that we are running the races of individu-als—of executives, teachers, students, retirees, factory workers, husbands, wives, patients, and parents, even pastors—who are seeking to survive in a difficult world. Yet those races are only one small part of the larger race as we conduct our lives as followers of Christ. When people look at us, they should see people who have been called by God to do whatever it takes to change the world by God's grace.

1. We become generous out of the natural overflow of thanksgiving in our hearts. What are ways you may open yourself up to receive the gifts of God's grace and love so that in turn your heart may be formed toward generosity? Are you receiving well? Why or why not?

2. What are your fears about relinquishing control of your finances to God? Lean into and name those fears by the power of the Holy Spirit. Ask God to set you on a trajectory of generosity and sacrificial love.

3. One of the themes of the early Church was that believers had everything in common. How might it look in our lives if we were to follow this counter-cultural example?

Body Building

"Then God said, 'Let us make mankind in
our image, in our likeness, so that they may
rule over the fish in the sea and the birds in
the sky, over the livestock and all the wild
animals, and over all the creatures that move
along the ground.' So God created mankind
in his own image, in the image of God he
created them; male and female he created
them. . . . God saw all that he had made, and
it was very good. And there was evening, and
there was morning—the sixth day."

—Genesis 1:26-27, 31

I have always been a person of good physical fitness. I played tennis and soccer and wrestled competitively until the age of twenty-two or so before I took up recreational basketball, golf, running, and cycling. I also played overly competitive dodgeball. No matter the sport, I always sought to maintain my physical fitness. There were times in my life when I prided myself on how "in shape" I was. Then I got injured.

At twenty-two, I had reconstructive surgery on one of my knees, and for the first time ever, I found myself unable to perform at the level to which I had grown accustomed. So I stopped performing. I stopped working out. I stopped competing, and to be honest, I stopped feeling like myself. When I began letting my body slip, a part of who I was created to be began to slip away with it. I was taking my body, the "very good" gift that God had given me, for granted. I no longer saw my life or my body for what it really was—a gift, an opportunity, and a means of revealing the glory of God.

Two years ago I began a new church in the urban core, and in the process I recommitted to getting back in shape. I was ready to go to work again. I joined a local gym. I tuned up my bike. I even bought a new pair of running shoes. Slowly but surely I have gotten back into decent condition. With that has come clarity of mind, more energy, confidence, joy, and self-discipline. Every time I run, I feel and think to myself, *This is why I was created.* The most important thing I've learned since starting back on this wellness journey is that my health and my faith are linked. As I've become physically fit once again, I've also drawn closer to God. When I seek to improve my physical body, my spiritual fitness improves as well.

Our bodies and our faith are not different parts of two separate worlds. I believe there is a connection. There is a direct correlation between our physical well-being, our faith, and our ability to live fully. The way we manage our physical health affects our spiritual well-being.

So, then, I'm curious.

How physically fit are you?

How spiritually fit are you?

Do you feel like yourself?

Do you feel like you are a new creation?

The missional life and our ability to live fully have much to do with practical disciplines such as worship and prayer, communion and companions. Without our bodies, however, we would not have much. Therefore, missional life is necessarily rooted in our physical bodies, our earthy, misshapen, unique, and at times limiting bodies. How we take care of our bodies and how we look at them is critical to our purpose and meaning. To start, let us take a look at the book of Genesis.

Very Good

In the beginning, God created the heavens and the earth. The earth was nothing more than a formless void. There was no shape to it at all. It was a blob of nothingness. Darkness covered everything. Then out of nowhere came the wind. The Holy Spirit swept over the face of the waters, over the nothingness, "and God said, 'Let there be light,' and [suddenly] there was light. God saw that the light was good" (Genesis 1:3-4).

God continued creating and naming, and in the process, God called everything he created *good*. First came the sky, then the stars in the sky. God made the land, the vegetation, all of the swimming things, and all of the creeping things. He looked at it all and said, "It's all *good*."

Finally God said, "Let us make humankind in our image, according to our likeness" (v. 26, NRSV). The Lord God then formed Adam, raising him from the dust of the ground and breathing into his nostrils. Man had become a living being. And like he had done so many times before, God took a step back and saw all that he had created. This time, however, God called it "*very* good" (v. 31, emphasis added). The same God who created the heavens and the earth created humankind. The same God who created the mountains and the valleys and the lilies in the valleys made you and me—created beings. We are creatures. According to Genesis we are beautiful creatures created in God's image. We, for better or for worse, are very good.

Our bodies are formed in a way that resembles the likeness of God. Our bodies reveal the glory of God. If ever we desire a glimpse of God, if ever we want to meet God, we simply need to look in a mirror, observe another in action, or watch in wonder as a child is born. Living missionally means remembering that we have all been created in God's image. Our physical bodies bear the image of God. Therefore, when it comes to missional living, caring for and maintaining our physical fitness will reveal God's image more clearly for all the world to see.

Understanding this is easy. Doing this is much harder than it sounds.

One of the things I have grown most thankful for about my wife is the way she takes care of her body. Wendy is a great steward of the gift she's been given. She is physically fit and more. Her healthy lifestyle serves as an extension of her faith. Her actions reveal that she believes, like the apostle Paul, that her body "is not some piece of property belonging to the

Missional life is necessarily rooted in our physical bodies: our earthy, misshapen, unique, and at times limiting bodies.

spiritual part of you [but that] God owns the whole works. So let people see God in and through your body" (1 Corinthians 6:19-20, TM).

The Garden

My wife maintains a strict diet of fruits, vegetables, and anything else that comes out of the earth (for those who are wondering, this includes meat but not dairy). Nothing she eats is processed. She adheres to 2 Corinthians, in which Paul writes, "Dear friends, let us purify ourselves from everything that contaminates body and spirit, perfecting holiness out of reverence for God" (7:1). In addition to maintaining a very simple diet, she lives a very disciplined life. She works out five days a week and balances her time between lifting weights and a cardiovascular regimen of running and circuit training. She keeps it simple. Building up her body is such a priority that, when given the choice between chocolate and fruit, Wendy chooses fruit. She prefers a trip to the apple orchard over a trip to Dairy Queen any day of the week. In fact, visiting apple orchards has become her favorite thing to do—especially when Honey Crisp apples are ripe.

Wendy and I tried to time it perfectly this year. We went on a date to the apple orchard in pursuit of Honey Crisp apples. When we arrived, the abundance of trees and the absence of people made it appear as if we were back in the garden of Eden. We were back in Genesis in the beginning and we were a modern-day Adam and Eve, walking hand in hand through a garden of apple trees. God was there with us as the tractor operator kept calling out the names of the trees from which we could eat and those from which we needed to stay away.

He shouted, "Jonagolds are to the left! You'll find McIntosh on your right! The Red Delicious are up a little ways, two rows in on the right!"

We anxiously awaited instructions about the Honey Crisps, but he never mentioned them. So we changed our minds at the last minute and hopped off the tractor near the Fuji trees and started in toward the approved "second place" trees. As we walked toward our apples, we stumbled upon two rows of unmarked trees.

We wondered simultaneously, "What are these? They look pretty good and they seem to be full of apples. I wonder why they aren't marked?" Wendy walked up to one of the trees and grabbed an apple that had fallen to the ground. She inspected it, looked at me, and whispered, "Scott, these are Honey Crisps."

We both stood still. We looked around to see if anyone else knew what we knew. My heart was beating a little faster. Hers was too. Here were two rows filled with the best apples in the orchard. Could it be that we were in heaven?

We looked around one more time to be absolutely sure that nobody was following us or watching us. We were alone, so I took a step closer and saw that these apples were indeed Honey Crisps. Then I hesitated and turned to Wendy.

"Wendy, I'm not sure we should pick these. They didn't tell us we could take them. They didn't even mention them. If they wanted us to have them, they would have said something, right?"

She replied, "Surely, they'd want us to have them. Honey Crisps are the best apples!"

And without warning, she picked one. She took a bite out of it, smiled, and said, "Scott, these are amazing!" Her delightful expression convinced me to do the same. I picked my own apple. I couldn't help myself. We couldn't control ourselves. The apples tasted so good. We ended up picking two bushels and, in the process, became prodigal in our decision making. Our vision was blurred. We had placed our character in jeopardy and had become bad stewards of the gifts we'd been given. Though we hadn't exactly defiled our bodies, we had certainly forgotten that the earth was the Lord's and everything in it, including but not limited to the Honey Crisps.

God created us, called us very good, and gave us dominion over all of creation. In those few moments, lured by the Honey Crisps, we had decided that these apples were ours and not God's. We could do whatever we wanted with them, and what we wanted more than anything was to eat them all up. We were tempted and lost control.

We ate so many apples that we actually made ourselves sick. This is how easy it is to stray from being the people we were created to be. This was not just Adam and Eve's story, but it's ours as well. This is ultimately the story of how we obscure the image of God and lose sight of who we are—namely, image bearers. We forget that we are the recipients of all of these amazing gifts, especially our bodies. God created us. He called us very good, and all God hoped for in return is that we take care of what we have been given.

Genesis 1:26 states, "Then God said, 'Let us make mankind in our image, in our likeness, so that they may rule over the fish in the sea and the birds in the sky, over the livestock and all the wild animals, and over all the creatures that move along the ground.'" We are made in God's image to take charge! We are created to manage all that we've been given. How we care for creation is what ultimately draws us nearer to

God and to each other. This trust is God's mission for us from the onset. Yet we often stray.

It did not take long for Adam and Eve to forget who they were. The moment they put their hands on the low-hanging fruit on the Tree of Knowledge of Good and Evil, God's precise trust was broken and a different image emerged. As a result, Adam and Eve could not see God's image any longer. Instead, they saw flesh, sin, shame, embarrassment, and limitation. Until Jesus (the second Adam) came.

On Christmas we celebrate the beginning of a new Eden: a new heaven, a new earth, and ultimately a new creation. Two thousand years ago God wrapped himself in human flesh to visit the earth as one of us. God became man that humankind might once again become like God. This is the whole idea behind the incarnation.

The God of the universe was born into this world as one of us to walk in our shoes in order that we might learn how to walk like God. Jesus is the bridge between humans and God. He is the way, the truth, and, ultimately, the life that allows us to live missionally and to become one with God and each other. Jesus was just like us.

The writer of Hebrews describes Jesus as a priest interceding: "For we do not have a high priest who is unable to empathize with our weaknesses, but we have one who has been tempted in every way, just as we are—yet he did not sin" (Hebrews 4:15).

How powerful it can be when we take the idea of incarnation seriously. God knows our weaknesses, understands them, and wrestled with temptations himself. When we come to him in prayer, we acknowledge one who has known hurt and heartache, weakness and disappointment, challenges and

HONEY CRISP

temptation. God is with us, is like us, and will always understand and empathize with us. This is good news of great joy, giving us hope for abundant life.

Jesus' life, death, and resurrection give us an opportunity to remember the almighty power of God who took on the flesh. His incarnation also gives us a chance to remember and resurrect the physical body in a way that once again reveals God's image to all of creation here and now. This is why Paul writes, "Therefore, if anyone is in Christ, the new creation has come: The old has gone, the new is here!" (2 Corinthians 5:17). Through the grace of Jesus Christ we are able to get back to the beginning. We are able to get back to that very good image of God in creation.

Laying Aside Old Clothes

For Christians, this begins in baptism. Baptism is a moment where by water and the Spirit we find new life; but in order to find new life, we must first experience death.

Do you not know that all of us who have been baptized into Christ Jesus were baptized into his death? Therefore we have been buried with him by baptism into death, so that, just as Christ was raised from the dead by the glory of the Father, so we too might walk in newness of life. For if we have been united with him in a death like his, we will certainly be united with him in a resurrection like his. . . . But if we have died with Christ, we believe that we will also live with him. . . . The death he died, he died to sin, once for all; but the life he lives, he lives to God. So you also must consider yourselves dead to sin and alive to God in Christ Jesus. (Romans 6:3-5, 8, 10-11)

Baptism is death. In baptism we are buried like Christ. We're immersed in water to a place where we literally cannot breathe in the breath of life. It is as though we were being buried. But by the power of the Holy Spirit we are raised to walk in the newness of life.

In the ancient church, baptismal candidates actually walked into the water as if they were marching in a funeral procession. They walked slowly in step one after another to the sounds of a pipe organ. As they emerged from the water, they would do so to the sounds of Easter choruses—because up from the grave they arose!

Baptism transforms us. It changes our lives. We're resurrected. And the same principle applies when it comes to managing our physical bodies. In order to build muscle, in order to sculpt and shape our bodies, we first have to tear down all of our muscle tissue. When we lift weights, exert energy, exercise our bodies, we are actually breaking down muscle. It is dying a little death. As we continue to alternate exercise and rest, our muscle tissue rebuilds itself, and as a result, it becomes stronger than it was before. In order to build muscle, we must first break it all down. In order to become a new creation, we must first die a spiritual death in baptism.

Have you been baptized?

Are you exercising?

Do you feel any different, physically or spiritually, when you exercise?

In order to fully receive the promises of God, we must experience a death like Christ's. We must die to the old in order to put on the new. I don't know what it was about my upbringing, but I never understood that process until a friend of mine invited me to church to witness his baptism.

I never knew this friend of mine was churched. Nothing about his life revealed that he was devoted to God. He was on my soccer team, where we both played defense. Together, we always thought of ourselves as being a little less than holy. We usually let language slip on the soccer field. We sometimes talked faster than we played. If anything, we were irreverent at best. Nevertheless, he invited me to his baptismal service.

I dressed up, made it to the church on time, and watched as they called him forward. He walked up to the front wearing soccer shorts and a T-shirt. As quickly as he stepped up, he stepped down into the baptismal font. The pastor standing behind the pulpit read a passage of Scripture in a way that brought out new meaning and significance for me. With a big voice he said,

> "Do you not know that all of us who have been baptized into Christ Jesus were baptized into his death? Therefore we have been buried with him by baptism into death, so that, just as Christ was raised from the dead by the glory of the Father, so we too might walk in the newness of life. For if we have been united with him in a death like his, we will certainly be united with him in a resurrection like his. . . . If we have died with Christ, we believe that we will also live with him." (Romans 6:3-5, 8)

Then the pastor took hold of my friend, and in one fluid motion, immersed him in the water and raised him up to a chorus of applause and Alleluias! The whole church broke out in excitement, and we sang together, "Up from the Grave He Arose." It was a powerful event. Unexpectedly, however, it left my friend and me with lots of questions.

After the service we walked home, primarily because he was soaking wet and had forgotten to bring a change of clothes. So we walked. As we did, we had a conversation I still remember.

My friend asked me, "Scott, did you hear what my pastor said?"

"Sure," I answered.

"Did he say that I died today?"

"I think so," I responded.

And then in true teenage fashion, my friend asked, "Does that make me a zombie? Am I now a part of the living dead?"

Chuckling, I replied, "Yeah, I guess so. I don't know."

He said, "I wonder if people will notice. Do you think people will notice?"

So my friend and I wondered together, "What does a person who has been raised from the dead look like? What does a person who has experienced a second birth look like? How do they walk? How do they talk? What kind of things do they do? Would their soccer teammates notice? What about their high school classmates? What about their parents?

That happened a long time ago, but years later my memory of that conversation with my friend was triggered. Last summer, a group of folks from my church were handing out water at First Fridays, a monthly community event in downtown Kansas City. At one point that evening, we were interrupted by a social club whose members were dressed like zombies. There were hundreds of them, shambling, groaning, and terrorizing the streets of Kansas City.

When I think of baptism and new life in Christ, I doubt that God envisions zombies. So what does actual new life look like? How can we live in such a way that we can bear the

Does that make me a zombie?

image of God in the hope that people will see our bodies, our lives, all of our good works, and know the glory of God?

When we think about the walking dead, most of us have an idea from Hollywood how they should look, smell, and feel. As clearly as we would recognize these Hollywood creations, we should be able to recognize those who are walking in the newness of life. We should notice those who are dripping wet with the waters of baptism, those who are soaked in the waters of new creation, and those who are gleaming with the light of Christ.

In the depths of our darkness, Jesus meets us where we are so we might be raised anew to walk with him on resurrection ground; in hope, in assurance, and in faith, God's promises assure us that the worst thing is never the last thing. Baptized Christians should look like people without fear, for they have already experienced death. John writes, "There is no fear in love. But perfect love drives out fear, because fear has to do with punishment. The one who fears is not made perfect in love" (1 John 4:18).

The book of Revelation paints new life a little differently. The author of Revelation says that the newness of life looks like a world where "'He will wipe every tear from their eyes. There will be no more death' or mourning or crying or pain, for the old order of things has passed away" (21:4).

We enter the baptismal waters by laying aside our old clothes, surrendering the former life of sin and death. Upon surrendering all we are and all we have, upon giving up control, we emerge then from the waters of death like newborn babes—innocent and blameless. We walk forward from that place wrapped in swaddling cloths of kindness, patience, humility, quiet strength, discipline, and the all-purpose garment of love.

We *should* look different when we become new creations. People should be able to see and know that we are different. This is what it means to be image bearers.

Do your friends know that you have been raised from the dead? When you look in the mirror, do you see someone who is bearing God's image?

Self-care

Obesity is one of the leading causes of preventable death in the United States. Being overweight is potentially lethal. In a recent study among United Methodist clergy living in North Carolina, it was discovered that obesity rates among clergy ranks more than 17 percent higher than the rest of the population. This is clearly a spiritual problem as well as physical problem. Worse, we seem to be passing down obesity to our children: statistics show that childhood obesity is becoming a growing epidemic. Is this reflecting God's image? Is this God's perfect love? Is this what Jesus had in mind when he was making all things new?

Jesus instructs the young attorney in Matthew, saying, "Love the Lord your God with all your heart and with all your soul and with all your mind." This is the first and greatest commandment. And the second is like it: "Love your neighbor as yourself" (Matthew 22:37-39).

This command has a number of implications for how we should live, but first and foremost it implies that we must love ourselves. We must take care of ourselves and be mindful of our bodies. To love your neighbor as yourself requires first that you love yourself. Great self-care enables us to live into God's greatest commandment in a fundamental way.

In Romans 12, Paul exhorts the church at Rome to offer their bodies as holy and living sacrifices. He commends to them a spiritual act of worship, living lives of sacrifice that are rooted first in the physical body. He expresses the idea that our bodies, and what we do with them, matter to God. They've been given to us as gifts—and gifts are meant to be returned to God's service, so that others might see our good works and know the glory of God.

How we treat our physical forms is very important. How can we steward our bodies in a way that reveals the power and glory of God and sets us free? Paul said, "I strike a blow to my body and make it my slave" (1 Corinthians 9:27). The key word here is "discipline." Caring for our body takes discipline. Starting and maintaining a proper diet and exercise program requires discipline. Again, Jesus said, "Love your neighbor as yourself." Often, we focus on the "neighbor" portion of this command and neglect the "yourself" portion.

It is important to schedule time to tend to your body routinely. For me, this has meant signing up for exercise classes or by finding a workout companion. Recently, my wife encouraged me. She said, "Scott, Paul writes in 1 Corinthians 7:4, that 'the wife does not have authority over her own body but yields it to her husband. In the same way, the husband does not have authority over his own body but yields it to his wife.' So I'm going to start taking authority over yours, and we're going to start working out together." We are now working out together three times a week at a gym. In the process, we have grown closer together in love by encouraging, supporting, and caring for each other's bodies.

Having said that, it's important to note that there is a delicate balance in motion when it comes to proper dieting and exercise regimens. It is easy to get carried away with matters pertaining to our physical bodies. Living fully is about striking a balance between several different dimensions of life and not obsessing over any given one or emphasizing one to the detriment of others. Christians should not obsess over their bodies to the point that it shackles them.

People should not turn what they eat or don't eat and what they do or don't do into a singular lifestyle. Exercise and diet should enhance our lives, not define them. Downtown Kansas City is home to a large vegan population. You might be wondering why I know this. The only reason I know it is because they are very vocal about it. In fact, it's almost as if their lives revolve around their diet.

Recently, I spoke to a vegan couple in my loft building, and it became obvious very quickly that their dietary practices are the focal point of their lives. In one ten-minute conversation, I heard about their week's worth of meals. Living fully is not about eating right for the sake of centering our lives upon food; it is about living in a way that will free us to meet and experience the living God. The missional life is concerned about diet to the degree that our dietary habits help us better encounter God, but no further. Obsession is just as unhealthy as addiction

Similar to diet, exercise has a tendency to become an obsession. Paul writes, "For physical training is of some value, but godliness has value for all things, holding promise for both the present life and the life to come" (1 Timothy 4:8). Even Paul recognized that caring for the body is important but not the mission or the focal point. There are far more important

to love your neighbor as yourself
requires first that you love yourself

things in life, namely our relationship with God and our neighbors.

On my wellness journey, I have discovered the importance of caring for my body, which I treat as a gift. When I take care of my gift, I find that I have more energy, time, and desire to pursue God. I have better clarity and insight. In addition, in the moments after I've gone on a long run, eaten a healthy lunch, or pushed myself to accomplish something I did not think was possible for me, I think, *God made me for a purpose, and I can see his pleasure on my face.*

God made us, limitations and all, in his image. God breathed into us the breath of life and called us very good. Today he calls us to maximize our gifts, offer them as living sacrifices, and bear the image of the One in whom and through whom others might see our good works and give glory to God in heaven.

1. Shara Worden of My Brightest Diamond sings, "I receive this body mine, from womb to grave." How might God be calling you to receive your body? How might he be asking you glorify him through your broken humanity?

2. As Scott Chrostek writes, to love your neighbor as yourself requires that you first love yourself. How might learning to treat yourself with more care result in better care and concern for others?

3. When God (Creator) made mankind (creature) he said, "It is very good." What are the theological and practical implications of agreeing with God in this sentiment? What are ways we may praise him in our creatureliness?

Living Fully:
Singing, Painting, Laughing,
and Dancing

Living fully, or pursuing God, means that we are living into the seven dimensions of the missional life that we've just journeyed through together. When we worship, love our neighbors, break bread together, read Scripture, pray, steward our money, and care for our bodies, we will find what we are looking for because we will see God wherever we go in all that we do.

Living missionally is seeing God everywhere we go in all that we do. It is learning how to praise God in all things. In working, in playing, at concerts and baseball games, in the mountains, and in the desert. We can even praise him at the pool.

Living a missional life requires that we search for God in all things and that we live into the heart of God by embracing and enjoying God's creative spirit everywhere we go. We were created in the image of God, and when our bodies move in concert with the rest of creation, we can fully reflect the beautiful and diverse image of our Creator God. Therefore, the missional life is rooted in searching for God's image, the glory of the Lord, in everything that has breath.

Seinfeld *and Snoop Dogg*

This past year my wife and I declared (just like George Costanza in *Seinfeld*) that the summer of 2011 was going to be "the summer of Scott and Wendy." We were going to live in a way that did not fear anything. We said yes to everything and tried to view all things as new opportunities to meet God. Each day we tried to do something new and adventurous.

We started with our stomachs and ate at a collection of eclectic restaurants, trying all sorts of different foods. We then gave our ears attention and attended several concerts. We then worked on our legs: we took up cycling for the summer, strolled through every park in Kansas City, and even attended an outdoor tennis match in the center of the city. Next, we turned to museums and musical theater. We toured the last remaining World War I museum. We visited several art museums and experienced dinner theater for the very first time. In each and every thing we did, we sought to look for God. We looked for him in different people, in different expressions of creativity, in new, unlikely, and exciting places.

I will not soon forget sitting in the front row at my first rodeo and bull riding competition. To see the awesome power of raging bulls and witness the courage of the cowboys holding on for dear life to a simple leather saddle was unbelievable. Watching a three-thousand-pound bull buck and kick, doing whatever it could to separate the rider from his saddle, gave me new insight into the responsibility we have over all of creation and how difficult a task that can actually be.

Wendy and I also attended a Snoop Dogg concert. We had not planned on attending, but on the day of the concert, we saw that tickets were still available while our other plans had fallen through. So we decided to give it a shot. The doors to the concert venue opened at 7:30 p.m., but Snoop Dogg did not arrive until shortly after 11:00 p.m. For three and a half hours, we waited; as we did, we talked with perfect strangers. We also ran into several unsuspecting future members of our young church.

I will never forget the look on Tom and Lucy's faces when they realized that their pastor had seen them at a Snoop Dogg concert. They were embarrassed, maybe even mortified, but it did not take too long before they realized that Wendy and I were there too. We were stuck with each other in a way

Snoop offered an unlikely benediction.

that neither of us anticipated. We were also bonded. When Snoop Dogg finally took the stage, we all enjoyed the concert together. We sang along to all the songs together. We relived the mid-1990s together. We enjoyed each other's company in a way that was freeing for all four of us. The surprising encounter showed us that God was at work, bringing us closer together with the people around us in the most unexpected of ways.

It is worth noting that as the concert ended, we looked at each other with considerable surprise when Snoop offered an unlikely benediction. He said to an audience of thousands, "Remember as you leave this place to live fully with peace, love, and soul." I don't know what we expected, but we did not expect to hear that, and probably no one in the audience did either. Dare I say it felt holy?

A few months later, I had the privilege of baptizing Tom and Lucy's first child. It was a beautiful moment. Not only did I feel as though I knew them fully, but they felt the same way about me. We were vulnerable members of an authentic Christian community who sought to pursue God without judgment, seeking the presence of God and neighbor everywhere—even at a Snoop Dogg concert.

I would like to say that was the only time we were surprised by God showing up in an unlikely place, but it wasn't. We also attended an Eminem concert that summer. We had not planned on attending that show either, but a few weeks before the show we received a pair of anonymous tickets.

Eminem put on a great show filled with energy and all the filthy lyrics we expected. Toward the end of his set, however, Wendy and I were surprised to witness Eminem cut the music, turn up the lights, and begin a confession. For five minutes, Eminem spoke of his battle with substance abuse and addiction. He talked openly about his recovery and the difficulty of the recovery process. We then sang together a gospel tune, of all things, and he closed the concert by asking us to sing two more songs with him.

As everyone joined in singing, it was as though a community was forming. Suddenly, this concert, filled with misfits and strangers, was transforming into one body.

We had confession. We heard the testimony of a life guided by a repentant heart. Then came the song we sang together, which was nothing less than a psalm of rage against slavery to sin and death. It was a song that ultimately proclaimed, "I'm not afraid, because we walk this road together." We were singing a song opposed to the fetters of substance abuse and addiction, and the chorus was nothing less than a psalm of reassurance. As Eminem spoke and sang, I began thinking about King David, the unlikely king who fell from power on account of his shortcomings and addictions. This is the kind of song that David would have sung: "Give thanks to the LORD, for he is good; his love endures forever. . . . The LORD is with me; I will not be afraid. What can mere mortals do to me?" (Psalm 118:1, 6). Even from the shackles of his sin, David found ways to sing. So did this crowd!

With over sixty thousand people in attendance, some of whom undoubtedly wrestle with substance abuse themselves, Eminem made himself vulnerable and pleaded for his audience to join him in singing and ultimately to join him on this journey of recovery in the hope that we might get through such issues together. As Eminem's message of confession, invitation, and communal chorus of repentance filled the air, I was moved. I could not process what was happening. I wondered, *What is going on here? This is not normal.*

Whatever was happening that night onstage, I certainly did not expect it. But I welcomed it.

Then the music changed. Eminem transitioned immediately into his closing song. If the people in the crowd weren't singing before, they were certainly singing as the music began. As Eminem was singing, it felt as though he had found what he was searching for. I, surprisingly, felt as though I had too. I was pursuing God, and I had met him listening to Eminem, of all people.

Everything Under Heaven

The author of Ecclesiastes writes, "There is a time for everything, and a season for every activity under the heavens" (3:1). This passage of Scripture reminds me that our limited time here on earth is going to be filled with all manner of unexpected and unplanned things. There is going to be a time for absolutely everything under heaven. There is a time for living, dying, weeping, and laughing; we have all experienced each one of these seasons and experiences. You may have even experienced all of these within the past few weeks or months.

Ecclesiastes also reveals that we cannot control any of these times—when they come or what they look like. We might work really hard to control or determine where we go in this life, but all of life's experiences rest inscrutably in God's unseen hands. Life will happen. It invariably does. Some life events are great and some of them are not—there is nothing we can do about it. The author of Ecclesiastes tells us that our lives cannot be mastered. There is a time for birth, for dancing, for laughing, for healing, for mending, for keeping, for peace, and for love; but for every one of those moments there is a time for its opposite. Our vision and how we see the world determine whether we will dance or fight.

When we live searching for God in the hope that we will experience the depth of his mercy and grace, we find that it is much easier to always dance. Living missionally is searching for and expecting to see God everywhere. It is looking for Superman in a world of Clark Kents. It is hoping for the potential Paul in every Saul. When we walk through life in this way, when we expect to encounter the living God everywhere we turn and remember God's perfect and pursuing love for humanity, we will realize that there is no reason to fear because we are never alone. God is always with us, and there is nothing we can do that will separate us from his love. In this way, every event, every season, and every experience becomes an opportunity for sacrificial love. We must go and do likewise, give everything we have and all that we are in the hope that others might see our good works, glorify God, and join us on the journey.

Communion Prayer

John Wesley, throughout his lifetime, sought to live fully and without fear. However, no matter what, he never felt completely assured. He felt as if he had more to offer. He wasn't doing enough. Even though he was baptized, educated, generous, and the founder of a Christian movement that would change the world, he continually feared. Shackled by his search for blessed assurance, Wesley sought to remember God's promise of perfect love; in so doing, he made a promise to God himself. This is also something that I do every morning.

Wesley, in the hope of living fully, prayed a prayer that shaped his life missionally. Wesley wanted to dance with the rhythms of life. He wanted to immerse himself in God's *we will dance or fight*

symphony of love. He wanted to feel it running through him. He wanted to sing to the melodies of God's love song. So he bowed down and prayed that he might hear, see, and live in perfect communion with both God and neighbor. He prayed that in all things he might be available to the presence of God. He prayed that he might see God everywhere he went. This was his prayer:

> I am no longer my own, but thine.
> Put me to what thou wilt, rank me with whom thou wilt.
> Put me to doing, put me to suffering.
> Let me be employed for thee or laid aside for thee,
> exalted for thee or brought low for thee.
> Let me be full, let me be empty.
> Let me have all things, let me have nothing.
> I freely and heartily yield all things to thy pleasure and
> disposal.
> And now, O glorious and blessed God, Father, Son and
> Holy Spirit,
> thou art mine, and I am thine.
> So be it.
> And the covenant which I have made on earth,
> let it be ratified in heaven.
> Amen.

Are you willing to pray this prayer?

We began this book by discussing an attorney who asked Jesus what he must do in order to find eternal life. What I have come to discover is that living fully is not an activity. It does not consist of a set of specific practices. It is a way of viewing the world in its many dimensions and then finding the courage to live into them wholly. It requires that we immerse ourselves in the seven dimensions of a missional life—half of which focus on loving God (worship, prayer, and the reading of Scripture), and the other half, which focus on loving our neighbors and ourselves (how we manage our money, how we manage our bodies, and how we turn strangers into friends).

The last remaining dimension manages to blend the two in a beautiful and mysterious way. God makes himself known to us in the breaking of bread. This is where the heart of God beats and breaks for us in a visible way; it is also where we come together with each other in a way that helps us remember that we are all created in God's image as his very good creation.

Jesus came to the earth that we would be filled with and employ God's perfect love. Jesus came that we would live as recipients of God's good gifts—without fear—and in so doing we would learn to love God and neighbor with everything we have. This is what happens in communion, and this is the heart of the missional life.

Paul writes, "Do nothing out of selfish ambition or vain conceit. Rather, in humility value others above yourselves, not looking to your own interests but each of you to the interests of the others" (Philippians 2:3-4). When we think of others as better than ourselves, we will find consolation in love. We will find joy and, ultimately, God. When we think this way and look at the world this way, we will finally be of one accord, of the same mind as Christ Jesus. Jesus had reason to give thanks to God always, even in the midst of his crucifixion.

"Though [Jesus] was in the form of God, [he] did not regard equality with God as something to be exploited, but emptied himself, taking the form of a slave, being born in human likeness. And being found in human form, he humbled himself and became obedient to the point of death on a cross" (Philippians 2:6-8). Even then he was able to think of others, and in doing so, he transformed an implement of death into a sign of life. As a result, "God also highly exalted him and gave him the name that is above every name, so that at the name of Jesus every knee should bend" (vv. 9-10). Through his life, death, and resurrection, Jesus became worthy of our worship and worthy of our thanksgiving. All that God desires is that we go and do likewise.

Joining in God's mission of perfect communion, loving God with our heart, mind, soul, and strength, and loving our neighbor as ourselves require all that we are and all that we have. It requires our whole being. It requires that we give of ourselves wholly in love and service. Our purpose as Christians is to love until the day when we become one with God, one with each other, and one in ministry to all the world. We must love until we experience altogether perfect communion.

I wish living fully were as easy as changing careers or moving into a new neighborhood. Living fully is about adapting our worldview in a way that looks for God and lives for God in all that we do, everywhere we go.

Jesus asks the young attorney who wants to live fully, "'What does it say in the scripture?' He replies, 'That's easy! You shall love the Lord your God with all your heart, and with all your soul, and with all your strength, and with all your mind; and your neighbor as yourself.' Jesus smiled and tells him, 'You have given the right answer; now do this, and you will fully live'" (Luke 10:26-28, paraphrased).

My prayer is that you will go and do likewise. If you do, you will find what you're looking for.

You shall love the Lord your God with all your heart, and with all your soul, and with all your strength, and with all your mind; and your neighbor as yourself.

Luke 10:27

JOURNEY THROUGH **THIN PLACES** WITH YOUR COMMUNITY:

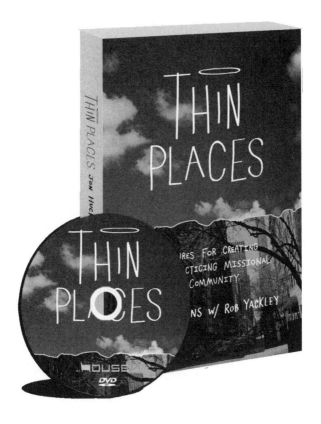

THIN PLACES: SMALL GROUP EDITION
Six Postures for Creating and Practicing Missional Community

Includes 6 Video Sessions with Jon Huckins, Rob Yackley, and members of their community.

To order go to thehousestudio.com

JOURNEY THROUGH **PUBLIC JESUS** WITH YOUR COMMUNITY:

PUBLIC JESUS: SMALL GROUP EDITION
Exposing the Nature of God in Your Community

Includes 6 Video Sessions with Tim Suttle

To order go to thehousestudio.com

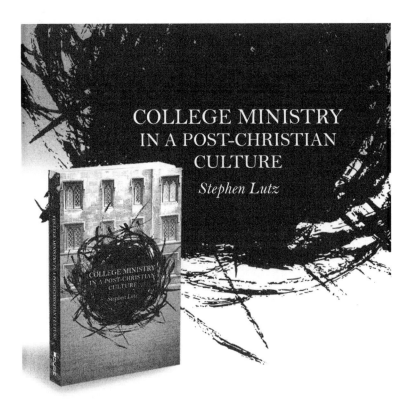